The Sacred Journey

by

Chris Surber

Energion Publications
P. O. Box 841
Gonzalez, FL 32560

ISBN10: 1-893729-85-0
ISBN13: 978-1-893729-85-8
Library of Congress Control Number: 2010940785

Energion Publications
P. O. Box 841
Gonzalez, FL 32560

(850) 525-3916
energionpubs.com

This work is for my fellow sojourners at

First Congregational Church

Peru, Illinois

I count it pure delight to share the pilgrimage of faith
in Christ with you!

Contents

"Blessed are the poor in spirit,
for theirs is the kingdom of heaven."
(Matthew 5:3)

"Blessed are those who mourn,
for they will be comforted."
(Matthew 5:4)

"Blessed are the meek,
for they will inherit the earth."
(Matthew 5:5)

"Blessed are those who hunger and thirst for righteousness,
for they will be filled."
(Matthew 5:6)

"Blessed are the merciful,
for they will be shown mercy."
(Matthew 5:7)

"Blessed are the pure in heart,
for they will see God."
(Matthew 5:8)

"Blessed are the peacemakers,
for they will be called sons of God."
(Matthew 5:9)

"Blessed are those who are persecuted because of righteousness,
for theirs is the kingdom of heaven."
(Matthew 5:10)

Foreword

Any journey that is to be undertaken requires choices whether the destination is to the nearest grocery store or on the other side of the globe. As Christians, however, we can embark on a sacred journey; it is that believer's pilgrimage that Pastor Chris Surber has so eloquently described through his reflections on our Lord's beatitudes (Matthew 5:3-10).

The reader will re-discover the totality of God's mercy, find reassurance in the totality of Christ's compassion and be humbled by God's unlimited grace. As Pastor Surber wrote, "...we are all broken. Recognition of this reality helps us to love, and not judge, one another. [It is] only when we recognize how deep our need is that we will know how vast is His love!" (p. 66). Be blessed by the journey you are about to undertake!

Karl W. Fivek, EdD

Peru, Illinois

Introduction

I once purchased a house in Tarpon Springs, Florida that prompted a fellow pastor to say of me that I was the kind of person who is willing to take something in shambles and rebuild it. As I immersed myself in the renovation of that old house his words rang more true than either of us could have known that day. The house had been recently remodeled inside but the outside property had much work left to be done. In Florida if a yard is left unkempt for more than about seven and half minutes it begins to turn into a suburban jungle!

For several months I worked the yard, removed bushes, planted healthy vegetation, installed stone, removed rock, painted decks, cleaned the pool area, and generally transformed the appearance of that once shabby abandoned jungle-yard into a lovely outdoor area. One scorching Florida summer afternoon I was in the front of the yard using an electric weed whacker to clean out some vines. While working I heard some kind of low growling sound. I turned off the tool and look behind me.

Apparently the pit-bull who was growling at me and showing his teeth was not fond of the sound of my gardening equipment! I have often wondered if I disturbed a lazy afternoon dog nap because he was so incredibly unhappy with me. I laid down my tool and extended my heavy leather glove covered hands in an effort to sooth the animal. This only prompted him to spring at me, stopping just short of my hands and baring his formidable teeth. With my heart leaping out of my chest, I began walking slowly backwards toward the back door of my house.

I was all the way on the front of my very rectangular property. The front door was locked so I knew that I had to make it all the way around to the back. Every few feet the dog would lunge at me and I would yell loudly. This would confuse him just enough to buy me a few more steps. It took me probably not more than a few minutes to make the walk around my property and into the back door of the house but it felt like a lifetime. After I was inside of the house I cracked the door to see if the dog was still on the back porch. When I opened the door he charged at the opening as if to get inside the house. I called the police who quickly dispatched a patrolman.

The police officer was able to "apprehend the suspect" by opening both of the back doors of his portal car, walking around the car while being pursued by the dog until the dog and he were eye to eye through the opened back doors of his car. He slapped the seat and the dog leapt into the backseat in attempt to get at the police officer. He quickly slammed the door and ran to the other side of the car to shut that door as well. The dog was taken away. I have never in my life seen anything more aggressive than that dog on that day.

I have never witnessed anything more determined, more insistent, more violent, or more singly focused on its target than that animal, that is with the exception of the radical love with which God pursues His creation! God in Jesus Christ was determined to make a way for sinners to be forgiven at the Cross. While man had sinned and caused a divide between himself and His creator, God has insisted that those who receive the grace and mercy offered in His Son shall be forgiven of sin and reconciled unto God in eternally secure love.

The violence of the love of God is shocking when we consider the brutality of the Cross. "He who did not spare his own Son, but gave him up for us all – how will he not also, along with him, graciously give us all things?" (Romans 8:32). The radical compassion of God is as compelling when we consider the wonder of the mercy of God. According to His perfectly just nature God demanded payment for sin. According to His perfectly loving nature He paid for our sin by sacrificing His own perfect Son.

2

God in salvation is singly focused on reconciling all who will place their trust, their faith, and their hope in that sacrifice. It is not we who make our way to God through good works, right belief, perfectly ordered creedal statements, or any other edifice of human composition. It is God who pursues us heatedly to receive the radical beauty of the violence of the Cross! "But he said to me, "My grace is sufficient for you, for my power is made perfect in weakness." Therefore I will boast all the more gladly about my weaknesses, so that Christ's power may rest on me." (II Corinthians 12:9).

God has pursued, forgiven, and reconciled us unto Himself. Through the wrath which was poured out upon Jesus, mercy was poured out on us. Salvation is purely the work of God's mercy and grace. We who have received Him have done so by faith when we have responded to the pull of God on our hearts. Grace rests upon us because God has loved us. What, in response to such a violent grace, should our reply to God be?

In what follows I have offered a collection of insights, thoughts, and personal experiences centered on and emanating from the Beatitudes of Jesus from the Sermon on the Mount. The Beatitudes offer a uniquely concise and complete understanding of the way of Jesus and the teaching of the Bible. Preaching and teaching them has had a profound impact on the shaping of my understanding of the sacred journey, the pilgrimage of knowing God in this life. The Christian life is not a onetime affirmation of any specific creed or faith statement.

The Christian life is a pilgrimage of encountering Christ as He is revealed in the pages of the Bible. The Christian life is about strapping on your sandals, picking up your walking stick, and following after the master of mercy – Jesus Christ! In the grip of His grace…

Pastor Chris Surber

Chapter 1

"Blessed are the poor in spirit, for theirs is the kingdom of heaven." (Matthew 5:3)

I spent two years living in Butte, Montana when I was a teenager. Butte is a small town nestled high in the Rocky Mountains. It lies in a small valley directly in the shadow of the great continental divide. This is a massive mountain range which stretches from New Mexico through Colorado. Its highest peaks extend through Wyoming, Idaho, and finally passing through and ending in Montana. The great divide may be seen from anywhere in the Butte valley. It is a marvel to behold with its snow covered peaks in the winter and panorama of green pine trees.

Easily seen from most parts of the Butte Valley is an immense statue which stands ninety feet tall at an elevation of more than three thousand feet on a mountain ridge above the city. The statue is more than eight thousand feet above sea level. It is a gorgeous statue named "The Lady of Rockies." The immense statue is in the likeness of Mary, the mother of Jesus. It was constructed in honor of women and especially mothers when it was completed in 1985. It was a nondenominational venture supported entirely by donations. It is a beautiful statue and is a great source of pride for the local people.

One summer my cousin Lee and I decided that we were going to walk up that mountain and touch that statue. Lee and his mother and sister had only moved to Butte a couple of months before. I had lived in Butte for a year but I had never given much thought to touching the statue. We decided to ask his mother to drop us off at the base of the mountain in about as straight a shot to the top as we could assess. We did so very scientifically, of course. We put our index fingers in the air and drew a straight line to what looked like a good spot!

She dropped us off fairly early the following morning with our backpacks loaded lightly with few bottles of water and a couple of sandwiches. We set out to climb the continental divide, a task which we assumed would take no more than a few hours and require little more than the breaking of a light sweat. As it turns out, the terrain which appears from the valley floor below to be a smooth mountainside is in fact riddled with crevices, cliffs, and giant rocky outcroppings of every variety. It took us nearly as long to get half way up as we had planned to be on the mountain all day.

At one point in our quest we both had the most ominous feeling that something was following us up the mountain. Convinced that it was a mountain lion we gathered large walking sticks to defend ourselves from the invisible beast which we believed to be looming only a few feet behind us in the brush in some direction. After several hours of climbing, we finally reached nearly to the top of the mountain. Through the trees we could see the gleaming white statue. I can still remember vividly the enormity and magnificence of that statue.

We eventually made our way through the trees and stood near the base of the statue. We were surprised to learn that what appeared to be a debris field of small stones beneath the base of the statue is in fact a graded field of immense boulders. The bolder field covers an area of several hundred feet beneath the statue. From the valley below the debris looks fairly unimpressive. Standing at this site the boulders are immense. They are a much greater obstacle than was first assumed by us, the explorers of misadventure!

Not to be deterred, we climbed those boulders as well. Finally we were less than forty or fifty feet from the statue but we were not to touch the statue that day or any other for that matter. The base of the statue is hewn flat with at least a fifty-foot rocky outcropping around the whole thing. There is no way to climb it short of professional climbing equipment. Despite all of our efforts we were thwarted by that mountain and did not reach our goal. We left in defeat, trudged down the mountain and made our way to rendezvous with my aunt. She eventually picked up the remains of the failed Lewis & Clark expedition.

Later that evening, one of my uncles asked us what we had been doing all day. After we told him of our adventure he informed us that we should have asked him to drop us off rather than my aunt because unlike my aunt who had only lived in Butte a few months, he would have taken us just a few miles from where we had been dropped off to a smooth road that leads right up to the statue from the back side of the mountain. Or, he explained through his laughter, if we preferred, he could have taken us to the local mall where they run bus tours by the hour!

While there are perhaps many lessons which could be gleaned from this story, I have always considered this a good example of the pitfalls of pride. Lee and I were strong, we were young, and we were both athletic and in great shape physically. We were also filled with pride. Rather than being humble enough to know that someone might have had helpful information about the mountain in front of us, we set out to climb this huge mountain our way. At the very least it would have been helpful to ask someone for a map! I am reminded of the words of Proverbs 12:15 "The way of a fool seems right to him, but a wise man listens to advice."

Pride is the great adversary of sound judgment. When faced with the mountains in this life, rather than humbly asking others for help we often rush off to disaster, heartache, or simply much unnecessary, fruitless work. Whereas pride is an obstacle to fruitfulness, growth, and success, humility is the smooth road to the top. At the end of the pathway of pride, no matter how successful we may be, we find a sheer cliff, impeding our ultimate progress. The pathway of humility is laden with the greatest treasure of all; knowing God.

I cannot say for sure why Jesus began the Beatitudes with an admonition toward humility. I can say for certain that pride is the greatest obstacle to knowing God, experiencing the sacred love of God in meaningful ways in this life. Perhaps Jesus started with humility because it is the place to start. The journey to God, the pilgrim path of following Jesus, starts at recognizing that this life is not primarily about this life and that it is not all about me. Love of self is the status quo of our day. Why is it that so many would-be converts and new believers stumble at the very beginning of the journey? The culture has convinced each one of us that my pleasure, my good fortune, and my happiness should be the center of my universe.

It is awfully difficult to surrender to the God of the entire universe when we see ourselves as the gods of each of our own little universes. When most of us think of humility we picture a little broken down, poor hermit with rags for clothes. Humility in the Bible is not a matter bringing ourselves low. It is a matter of exalting God for all that He is. Humility is not self-condemnation. It is seeing ourselves for who we really are, in our brokenness, and seeing God for who He really is, in His splendor!

I remember once when I was about sixteen years old and living on my grandmother's couch. I enjoyed a fairly humble existence with my afghan to keep me warm and a pillow, both of which I would neatly fold in the morning and place under a coffee table so as to remove any knowledge of my having slept there the night before. She had given me a dresser in the garage so that I had a place to keep my clothes and to tell you the truth, I felt incredibly blessed to have any of it. The alternative was to return to life with my alcoholic father back in Butte.

I had recently been drawn to the overwhelming love of Christ by the sweeping power of the Holy Spirit in this sinner's life. I had recently encountered Christ though it is much more accurate to say that He had encountered me. He had broken into my life and radically altered my experience of the world, my hopes, my dreams,

8

my aspirations. I had only begun to study the Bible but it didn't matter. I was desperately in love with my Savior. I had known life without God. I had known pain and emptiness. Now the love of God had taken up residence at the very center of my soul and I was lost in sacred love, covered, basking in divine sovereign grace.

On this particular evening my younger cousin Phillip inquired of my new found faith in God. I have lots of cousins! I had told him of my conversion to Christ. He had seen the drastic change in my attitude and demeanor. He knew that I had completely changed how I spent my time. He asked me why I was now spending so much time reading the Bible. I told him that it contained the words of life. He then asked the real question that I think all of us are asking in one form or another. "Why do you pray to a God that you cannot see?" "Why do you worship Him?"

I gave him the rather rudimentary illustration that I humbly offer to you now. Years of formal theological study, countless books read, and hundreds of sermons preached and this simple illustration still stands out in my mind. I had just made a meager snack of creamy peanut butter spread over some generic brand saltine crackers, neatly stacked and arranged on a cheap paper plate. Holding one of the pre-peanut-buttered crackers in my hand I proceeded with a dazzling apologetic.

A saltine cracker is easily one of the cheapest food substances, per item, available at a grocery store. For barely one dollar plus tax a person can purchase a box which contains four packages of about twenty five crackers. That is basically one cracker for every penny spent. There is nothing particularly unique or beautiful about any of those crackers. In fact, if it were not for the salt on the crackers they would have almost no flavor at all.

God is beyond anything in the entire universe. His beauty is far too great for us even to fully imagine. His glory is too splendid for our human eyes to behold and far too vast for our hearts to conceive. He is worthy beyond measure. Compared to the uniqueness of God I am no more unique than any of those crackers is when compared to me. I went on to tell him that it is not that I am unworthy, it is that He is so infinitely full of worth and that in spite of my simplicity, sinfulness, and selfishness He has showered me with love and grace! I worship not because my lowly state necessitates that I worship something. I worship God because of His immeasurable worth. I am able to worship Him because He did not abandon me in my lowly state. He did not leave me in my brokenness. I worship Him because He is so completely full of worth and, had He done nothing for me directly, He would still be worthy of worship because of who He is. However, having been rescued from the emptiness of this life by His mercy, I worship Him because I love Him. I don't expect the cracker illustration to soon become an offering in any preaching resource helps book anytime soon. However, it made its point that evening and I trust that it does for you now.

Why the beatitudes? The principles of the Sermon on the Mount are often referred to as the beatitudes; a phrase derived from the Latin word *beatus*, which means a state of blessedness or happiness which is not contingent upon outward circumstances. The pure spiritual life of the Christian is rooted in the love of God which He has showered upon us in Jesus Christ. "There is no fear in love. But perfect love drives out fear, because fear has to do with punishment. The one who fears is not made perfect in love. We love because he first loved us" (I John 4:18-19).

If we are to find ultimate satisfaction in this life it will not come from material possessions, being good people, or achieving a great many things. Even the best of these sorts of things with the greatest of intentions will never have the power to satisfy us fully. Only the love of God has the power to fully bring satisfaction in the depth of our beings. At the unshakable core of pure satisfaction is found a heart that is filled with the love of God. Love of accomplishments, even good, well meaning, useful accomplishments, is really only love of self.

When I was a young Marine I was consumed with achievement. Having come from fairly humble beginnings, I had great plans for my present and my future. I worked hard and as a young man, I had an above average military career. In my mind all of my military training and experience in the Marine Corps was preparation for a life of making money in the business world, though God had other plans.

I recall when a close friend and fellow Marine married a woman whose father was a very successful business man in San Diego, California where we were stationed. On the afternoon that I met my friend's future father-in-law I entered into a conversation with this man about my hopes and dreams of one day achieving a life similar to that which he had achieved. He told me something that has had a profound impact on the way in which I viewed success ever since then. I understand it and live it out much more fully now than I did then. He said, "I consider myself not to be successful now because I live in an expensive house and have lots of money. I am successful now because I enjoyed every step of the journey."

Satisfaction in this life is not a goal to be reached as if it were a pot of gold at the end of the rainbow. Satisfaction comes in being yielded to God every day of the journey. Our ultimate satisfaction does not lie in the things we gain in this life. If your source of peace is stuff, accomplishments, or accolades, you will never achieve peace. There will always be another hurdle to jump, hill to climb, or thing to get. True satisfaction comes from living daily yielded to God.

Our temporal happiness is rooted in God's eternal love for us. Our daily joy is found daily. Joy is not the promise of a life which has been well lived. It is the natural byproduct of living submitted to God in each day, in each moment. Humility is the starting point of the journey of encountering the divine love of God. It is not until we set aside our pride, our accomplishment-seeking love of self that we are able to see God in His fullness. In other words, we get in the way of getting the very thing that we are seeking.

We want approval but fail to find it because we seek it from the world around rather than finding it in super abundance in the love of God. We seek peace in the innermost parts though pride of accomplishment only to fail at attaining peace because our accomplishments only feed our love of self. Peace, hope, and joy, are found in the process of letting go of our ego-driven self-embrace as we are encircled by the loving arms of our Heavenly Father. Being "poor in spirit" means that we completely exalt God in our lives to the exclusion of self-exaltation.

"My heart is not proud, O LORD, my eyes are not haughty; I do not concern myself with great matters or things too wonderful for me. But I have stilled and quieted my soul; like a weaned child with its mother, like a weaned child is my soul within me" (Psalms 131:1-2). Pride is the enemy of the sacred. Humility is the doorway to finding freedom in the love of God through Christ.

The Pilgrim path that Jesus outlines in the Beatitudes is not the path for salvation. It is the path of those who are saved by faith in Christ to live out their saving faith. Salvation, kingdom citizenship, comes by faith in Jesus Christ according to the overwhelming grace of almighty God. What I am talking about here is not how one becomes a citizen of the kingdom of heaven but how we grow in our knowledge of the king! I have been a citizen of the United States my entire life but I have never met the president. The kingdom of heaven is completely paradoxical to even the best earthy kingdom. We have been granted the privilege of not only meeting but daily dining with the king.

Jesus is right now calling out to you and me, "Here I am! I stand at the door and knock. If anyone hears my voice and opens the door, I will come in and eat with him, and he with me" (Revelation 3:20).

The Sermon on the Mount is Jesus' inaugural address. In it He explains what He expects from His followers. Jesus' words echo those of Proverbs 16:19 where it says, "Better to be lowly in spirit and among the oppressed than to share plunder with the proud." Pride is an affront to God but lowliness of spirit is a precursor to knowing God. Humility is the pathway of the righteous because it is not until we get out of our own way that we are able to see God in the fullness of His beauty and worth!

I am reminded of the gold watch that I found as a young boy. I found it covered in dust in a box buried deep in our garage. I decided to take it apart to see what was inside. I couldn't get inside by more conventional means so I smashed it with a hammer and all of the parts went flying. In my efforts to see what was inside I completely destroyed the watch. Only after what I had done was discovered by an adult, did I discover – very much to my disliking – that the watch was an antique made of solid gold. It was priceless and in my honest ignorance I destroyed its worth.

Pride stops us from discovering the ultimate worth of God because when we are consumed with our own supposed worth, we become blinded to the immeasurable worth of God. We are our own worst enemy. God offers His love but we don't experience it in its fullness because we are consumed with self love. We become unto ourselves the tall person in a nearly empty movie theater who just has to sit right in front of us! How tragic it is that the greatest enemy to our fully experiencing the sacred presence of God's love in our hearts is our own pride.

Man has the distinct inability to save himself. Humanity in general, and each one of us in particular, is in the precarious position of having neither the means nor the ability to save ourselves. We can do nothing to affect our own sinful condition. Yet the personality of humanity is marred with pride. We are as the fool who has gambled all of his money away at the casino and then audaciously offers investment advice to a wealthy neighbor. In the beatitudes Jesus is offering a pathway to the sacred which is centered completely on God. This He juxtaposes with the more typical fleshly ways of attaining of the pseudo-blessings of our own making.

From the very beginning man has attempted to save himself, to exalt himself, to glory in his own strength. This is the message of the account of the Tower of Babel in the Old Testament.

Genesis 11:4 says, "Then they said, 'Come, let us build ourselves a city, with a tower that reaches to the heavens, so that we may make a name for ourselves and not be scattered over the face of the whole earth." We are always trying to make a name for ourselves rather than exalting the name of God.

People are just as busy building towers today. If we are honest we would have to say that we have a few towers in our lives. Each one of us, to varying extents, is equally guilty of the very same thing. Every day we have a decision to make. Whose glory will we see? Who will we crown today?

Several years ago I took to the habit of calling my wife "Princess." While there are some women who wear such a title out of vanity or pride. I granted her that title as a constant reminder that she is a daughter of the king. For me it was a way to remember her intrinsic worth as the king's daughter. A great weight and worth of the title of a princess is not found in her alone. While a princess may be incredibly valuable, beautiful, and worthy in her own right, her ultimate worth comes from the title of her father. Likewise, our ultimate worth does not come from who we are but from who our Father is. When we humbly find our ultimate worth in the glory of our Heavenly Father rather than finding our ultimate worth in our own prideful view of self, we unchain the entry to the pathway of encountering the sacred in our lives.

Does God seem afar off? Does the love God sound only like a nice idea or poetic language flung from the pulpits of churches? The first step on the sacred journey is the stripping away of pride. It is the greatest and first impediment on the journey. It must be done daily. It must be done continually. There is no more constant enemy of knowing God than our own pride. It gets in the way of our marriages. It destroys families and blocks our relationship with our children. It also clogs the works of the primary relationship in our lives – that of knowing our creator. There is a God. He is not silent. He longs to be known.

We must answer the questions, "who will be crowned this day as the king of our life? Which path will we follow this day?" Will we pick up the crown of pride, the crown of self-reliance, the crown of self-exultation, and do it our way or will we take our crown and place it squarely at the foot of the throne of God's grace? Then, as we travel the distance of the day at hand, in each moment, in each decision, in each situation that we face, will we make Christ King or ourselves?

I remember one evening when I lived in San Diego, California. The imagery of that misty cool winter night in Southern California is as vivid now as it has ever been. I was in the middle of a trial in my life. I felt alone. I felt betrayed and abandoned by people and by God. I drove my rust-worn Toyota from my apartment in Vista to the beach in Oceanside, California. I parked the car and walked out onto the beach. I noticed that someone had been busy that day building a sand castle.

To refer to this monument in the sand as though it were an ordinary sand castle is a grave sort of injustice to this masterpiece in the sand. It was at least six feet high and at least twice that in circumference. It was as massive as it was detailed. It had a moat, several towers, and each brick was carefully outlined with magnificent detail. I sat down on the cold sand nearby. As I examined this masterpiece of craftsmanship I realized that the tide was starting to come in. I watched that evening as the mild but steady ocean waves washed over and completely destroyed the labors of someone's hands. What had no doubt taken an entire day to create was washed away completely in just a few minutes.

Proverbs 14:12 says that "There is a way that seems right to a man, but in the end it leads to death." What sand castles are we building? Consider your own motives. In every moment of our lives the matter of kingship, humility, and pride is at stake. In this decision which faces me right now in this moment, who is king? Will my pride prevail or will I humbly submit to the will of God in this situation? The bigger picture of our lives is composed in these individual decisions.

When I choose career over family in a given moment and do so again and again it becomes my pattern of behavior and eventually it becomes the theme of my life. The same may be said of an inexhaustible list of other examples. When I was a teenager I boxed for a couple of years. To be honest with you, I was never very good. I won a few fights but lost a lot of fights, too. I learned a lot of lessons the hard way through my short career as an amateur fighter. I learned a lot about humility.

They say in boxing that you usually learn a lot more from a loss than a win. When you win a fight you tend to be more concerned with celebrating the victory than with learning from what you did wrong. I also learned another valuable lesson. I learned about muscle memory. When you throw a punch a certain way one thousand times you will throw it that way for the rest of your life. Indeed, to this day if I hit a punching bag the style and technique of my punches is very much the same as it was when I was a sixteen-year-old amateur boxer. The same principal applies in every area of our life.

When we consistently judge others rather than love them, we train our internal spiritual muscle memory how to respond to people. When we routinely make decisions that exalt our needs, our wants, our desires, over the needs of others and the exaltation of God in our lives, we train our minds that we wear the crown. The beautiful thing is that the opposite is equally true as well. The sacred Scriptures admonish us to "Have nothing to do with godless myths and old wives' tales; rather, train yourself to be godly. For physical training is of some value, but godliness has value for all things, holding promise for both the present life and the life to come" (I Timothy 4:7-8).

Whenever I am at the gym working to lose the extra energy storage cells around my midsection (fat), I marvel at how much people on treadmills look like hamsters on exercise wheels. The level of dedication on the part of so many people in our culture astounds me. They run and run and run and go nowhere. They climb and climb and climb on stair-stepping machines and never leave the first floor! If we trained our minds and spirits the way

16

that we train our bodies, we would be so saturated with the sacred reality of God's love that it would be palpable to the world around us. Training is not reserved for athletes.

If we are to know the reality of God's glorious reign in our lives, then we have got to train ourselves to submit to Him humbly, moment by moment. Do you long to know God in fuller and deeper ways? Train yourself to submit the very intentions of your heart, the thoughts of your mind, to Him humbly, one moment at a time. This is the pathway to knowing God. The power of God is unavailable to the proud because Christ is king and will not share His reign with a prideful heart. There is not enough room for His genuine authority and my rebellious nature in one human heart.

The torrent of God's love is so vast and complete that as it floods our hearts it necessarily chases away all else. To be a child of God means that the light of Christ invades every dark corner of your life. There is no such thing as an action that it not associated with the Lord's will for a child of God. When Jesus is king, he requires that his entire domain is under His rule. We love God by submitting to one another in our marriage. We worship God as we humbly see to the needs of those who are in need in and around our lives.

To be poor in spirit means that we are as beggars who rely completely on the good graces of others for our sustenance. We recognize that all that we have, all that we are, and all that we ever hope to be is the gift of God's grace. To move forward on the sacred journey of knowing God and living as Jesus' disciple, we must begin with this understanding of ourselves and God. Such an understanding will not transform us overnight. However, it will unlock the gate which leads to the pilgrim path. Faith is the key that turns the latch.

This matter of kingship in the Christian life must not be overlooked if we are to be people of the Pilgrim's path; if we are to be people of the way of the Kingdom. At their very core, sin, selfishness, and pride are about kingship and these are the things which stop us from having deeply satisfying relationships with God. Pride is the cliff separating us from God, even at the end of a long and arduous journey. Sin is the lion following us on our path, seeking to devour us as it ensnares and traps us within it cruel grip, its teeth tearing us to shreds even as its lips entice toward it with promises of earthly pleasure, satisfaction, and happiness. Earthly happiness, the shallow sort of peace that the world offers through sin, never lasts because it is based on outward circumstance, but *beatus*, the happiness that it is offered through humble submission to Christ is not contingent upon outward circumstance. Happiness is based on happenings; genuine and lasting peace is based solely and completely upon Christ.

Jesus said, "Peace I leave with you; my peace I give to you; I do not give it to you as the world does. Do not let your hearts be distressed or lacking in courage" (John 14:27 NET). Pride is the rocky outcroppings impeding our path just as much as it is the prevailing and dominating factor in our inability to crown Christ as King; to make Him not only Savior but Lord of our life. Jesus is not only sweet Savior. He is also sovereign Lord and King. Pride is a dark fog covering the mountain obscuring our view of Christ. It is the dark fog in our hearts keeping us ever-looking inward when we ought to be ever- and only looking unto Christ!

Humility then is primarily about making Christ King because humility is not about seeing ourselves in a lowly stature but seeing Christ in all of His supreme beauty, majesty, and worth. Humility is ascribing the unsurpassed worth to Christ and in so doing, crowning Him King of our lives. Humility has absolutely nothing to do with devaluing oneself, as it is often misunderstood, and everything to do with valuing Christ. We are God's creation and of immense worth and value. God made His creation and called it good. He sent Jesus and said that He was His beloved son in whom He is well pleased. Then, by the adoption we have received through faith in Jesus Christ, the Bible says that we have become sons and daughters of God. A diamond is of incredible value, but it is nothing compared to the one who made it. You and I are of immense worth, but our ultimate worth flows from the one who made us.

Dear saints of God, may you be encouraged, this very day, to set aside the destructive power of pride and commitment to your own strength, knowledge, and power. These things are fleeting but Christ is eternal. Lay down the pride which impedes you along the stony trails of this life in favor of that thing which places you in the greatest position to receive the overwhelming blessing of knowing God along the journey; a humble appreciation for who you are in the light of who He is. I am reminded of the words of the classic hymn, "On Christ the solid rock I stand, all other ground is sinking sand; all other ground is sinking sand" (Edward Mote).

My wife, Christina, and I are passionate supporters of the special needs community in our area. A dear friend of ours coaches and manages a local softball league which is just for special needs children of various social, mental, and physical levels of functioning. We routinely take our children to watch the games at a local park. Our family knows and loves many of the children present. My son, Sebastian, is a real sports fan. His little brother, Ephram, on the other hand, is a much greater fan of the concession stand!

On this particular evening then three-year-old Sebastian was glued to the game as he sat high in the bleachers, cheering for the dedicated players. Sebastian loves to cheer for his friends. Once Ephram had grown weary of the game and ran out of popcorn, he needed new avenues of adventure. He and I went for a walk to see what was happening at the other two baseball diamonds.

On one of the other fields there was a group of very athletic and talented young men playing baseball. The pitcher was throwing the hardball at great speeds, the batters swung their bats with impressive intensity, and the fielders pounced on ground balls as tigers do their prey. It was really a grand affair. On the next field there was a group of young women playing an equally forceful game of fast pitch softball. These two games went on while back at our game Sebastian sat watching in his typical high-spirited fashion, clapping for every hit, and bouncing excitedly when anyone on the field made or even attempted to make a play.

The children playing in the game which Sebastian watched were kids from across the full spectrum of developmental and physical disabilities. While their abilities and personalities are very diverse, they all had one thing very much in common. Just like the young men and women on the other fields, they came to play! In this game everyone got to hit the ball, everyone got to make it to first base, and everyone got to round the bases. I would venture to say that the level of enthusiasm, comradery, and sportsmanship on that field rivaled any other game taking place in any field anywhere.

That evening watching the gentle spirit of these ballplayers reminded me that it is not always about winning and losing. In fact, I would suggest to you that life is seldom, if ever, primarily about winning and losing. It is not even about "how you play the game," though surely that is important. Success and a lack of success in this life is largely a matter of perspective and how one defines the terms. What does it mean to be successful? Does it mean that the person who hits the home run and rounds all of the bases is the most successful?

Perhaps in softball that is what it means but if we apply this attitude, this perspective, to our lives then we are very likely to win the wrong game. Ultimately, what God has offered us in this life is a new perspective. No longer are we bound to the world's understanding of worth and value. Our Savior does not measure a person's worth in terms of accomplishment and achievement. As we embrace faith in Jesus Christ, the Bible says that the old is passed away, we are new creations, and that we are born again. Those who are found alive in Jesus Christ should have a different perspective.

Every one of the many special needs people in my life have taught me the most valuable lessons I have yet learned. In the game of life, sometimes just spending time with your friends as you each take turns rounding the bases is more than enough to equal success. Our lives are indeed often too cluttered, too busy, too loud, and don't make much sense. Our priorities are very often out of sync with what matters most. In God's economy, it is the humble that are exalted and great. Why? It is precisely because God is able to reign in their lives in simplicity and honest humility. The beauty of the love of God cannot blossom in the stony seedbed of pride.

In the book of Acts we read of the conversion of the Apostle Paul. Though he was a man very far from the truth of Jesus Christ, the Bible says that after having encountered the risen Jesus and subsequently having placed his faith in Him, "Immediately, something like scales fell from Saul's eyes, and he could see again. He got up and was baptized" (Acts 9:18). Dear child of God, today the sovereign God of the universe is calling you to lose the scales from your eyes.

He is calling you to embrace faith in His Son Jesus Christ that you might usher in a new perspective in your life. Humility is the first step toward knowing God's love personally as it penetrates our souls and crushes our pride.

Chapter 2

"Blessed are those who mourn, for they will be comforted."
(Matthew 5:4)

The words of the second line of the Beatitudes may be one of the most paradoxical sayings of Jesus in the gospel accounts. Blessed are those who mourn? Even if I will be comforted how is my mourning in any way blessed? Likewise, this may be one of the most weighty statements that Jesus ever spoke. As with all of the sacred Scriptures, it is filled with relevance for today. Life is both filled with sorrow and joy. God's love is not defined by how much He lavishes us with joy. God's love is perfect because He is perfect, not because we are always perfectly happy.

Growing up in Northern California in the 1980s my mind was filled with all sorts of vague, indistinct notions about what mattered most in life. The constant postmodern drumbeat of "finding the truth within me" seemed as shallow then as it does now. I was a confused kid. My father had left when I was very young. My family operated on a hazy kind of morality which was centered on the idea that what anyone did was just as acceptable as what anyone else did. The central value was simply not to hurt anyone directly by your behavior.

I am a child of this age. I was taught indirectly by the culture and directly by many people in my life that what matters most is having fun and being "happy." Is happiness all that really matters in this life? What about the man with a terribly indistinguishable Christian faith, in my first pastorate, who was fond of saying that "it's all about having fun" with regard to nearly everything which was being discussed? Is it all about having fun? The commonly held assumptions of our age affirm this philosophy.

The social and religious schizophrenia of our age astounds me. On the one hand we run at a near fevered pace in our constant pursuit of present entertainment and happiness. On the other hand we ignore the reality of the brokenness of life. Is it really surprising that so many people are filled with anxiety and depression when they are bombarded by the incessant lie that they are supposed to be always happy? There are things in this life which bring us to our knees. There are pains in this life that crush us to the core of our being. Outward happiness often masks broken hearts which have never been allowed to grieve.

What of the times when you throw your burden-filled prayer to the throne of God and in reply hear only the echo of your own crying voice? Are you supposed to be happy then? The sacred journey, the pilgrim path, is often, and not occasionally, a tedious journey filled with sorrow and heartache! O, how the heart of this shepherd is pained by the likes of the modern prosperity preacher! He tells Christians that their best days are always and necessarily just around the corner. It may in fact not be so. In Lamentations the Scriptures attest "Joy is gone from our hearts; our dancing has turned to mourning" (5:15).

What of the man and woman whose child dies unexpectedly just weeks after birth? Is their best life now? What of the wife whose husband dies of wounds inflicted during military service overseas? Would the outcome have been different had she prayed more fervently or perhaps if they had sent in more to the prosperity preacher on television? While we will deal more directly with the modern prosperity gospel in chapter eight, suffice it to say that grief, sorrow, and pain are all a part of the natural processes of this life.

When we mask the pain of this life, we become like the man who refuses to go to the doctor to have his wound treated. At first his limp is almost unnoticeable. After a while he is barely able to hide his pain and his altered gait. Eventually the infection is so severe and deep seated that his unwillingness to seek help becomes his usher to the grave. How many believers have broken hearts which hide behind the veil of outward happiness? Sorrow is not foreign to the life of the believer. It was not foreign to the life of Christ. The shortest verse in the Bible reminds us simply of a simple truth. Jesus was no stranger to the real sorrow of life. What was the response of our Lord to the death of His friend Lazarus, who He ultimately raised from the dead? "Jesus wept" (John 11:35).

Tears are not the empty vessels of human weakness. They are the containers of our pain which flow like a river toward the throne of God's mercy and grace. Why are those who mourn blessed? They are blessed strictly because it is God who will comfort them. In other words, our mourning will turn to joy as we turn our hearts over to the Lord. Comfort has a source. Some find it in the hallow consolation of alcohol abuse. Others find it in the temporary escapes of carnal desires or the excitement of spending money that they may not even have to spend!

How foolish it is to bury our pain beneath the facade of outward happiness when healing is available and is offered so freely from the hand of the Most High! God, even now, beckons you to receive the overwhelming flood of His healing love and grace. First we must recognize that we have a need for His healing. We must allow ourselves to mourn so that our hearts will be softened in order to become receptive to His love. Only the person who recognizes their tremendous need for comfort will open their mournful heart up to the love of God.

When I was a young Marine I was very concerned with the outward appearance of things. In fact to this day I keep my hair nearly in regulation, my dress shoes shine, and my pants have a crease. In the Marine Corps the appearance of your uniform is the first thing that is seen. Your outward appearance, the state of your uniform, tells your superiors how motivated you are as a

Marine. When a young Marine is inspected, the sergeant will often pass right by, with very little examination if that Marine's uniform is properly pressed and without outward blemish. One of the techniques which we often used to give a great outward appearance was to remove the buttons on the breast pockets of top "blouse" of the camouflage uniform.

The buttons would be removed and fastened tightly down with super glue. That way when the uniform top was heavily starched and neatly pressed there would be no button outlines on the outside of the pocket flap. This gave a little extra pizzazz to the appearance of the uniform. It also rendered the pocket completely useless. While in garrison this was not of great concern. The pockets were seldom used. When a Marine was in more serious field training the pockets looked good but actually hindered a Marine's ability to use the uniform to its fullest functional capacity.

We can dress up our appearance. We can carefully mask our pain with a counterfeit smile. When the next storm rages in our lives though, we will find our heart likewise unable to fully cope with the pressures of the situation. In other words, just because something looks good on the outside doesn't mean it is good. Rather than masking our mourning, the love of God compels us to run and not walk to the shelter of the Cross of Jesus Christ! He has poured out mercy in abundance. "You turned my wailing into dancing; you removed my sackcloth and clothed me with joy" (Psalms 30:11).

The heart that worships God through its tears worships Him in honesty. This is what Jesus is saying in John 4:23 when He says, "Yet a time is coming and has now come when the true worshipers will worship the Father in spirit and truth, for they are the kind of worshipers the Father seeks." God is not unfamiliar with our pain. Bring it to God to use for His sovereign purpose. Only when we acknowledge our brokenness can we get our pride out of the way for God to move in our lives.

Conjure in your imagination, if you would, a time in your life when the circumstances of your life were particularly troubling.

Think of a time when your heart was filled with worry, grief, or sorrow. With regard to people what comes to mind? For me I think of the ones who stood by my side and the ones who left. When our life is going well people seem to be attracted to us like magnets to metal. When things crumble we often find ourselves alone. In Romans 12:15 the Apostle Paul tells us to "Rejoice with those who rejoice; mourn with those who mourn."

It is true that we must bring our brokenness before God like an offering of all that we are to His service, for His healing power to work in our lives. Those who hide their mourning are not at all likely to find healing. It is buried, locked away in their hearts. It is shackled in chains of despair, guarded by souls which long for comfort but will not bring its wounds to the great healer. When we bring that brokenness to God He often – most often – works through the hands of another person to effect healing.

I realized very early on in my work as a pastor that I do not have answers for every question. Even the greatest of Bible scholars must accept the reality of their own finitude. To fail to recognize one's own inability to answer all of the questions of life is to be steeped in pride, not wisdom. Sandy was a woman steeped in despondency. Her husband had abandoned her after a long and tumultuous marriage. He had seldom been faithful. He left her under the crushing weight of financial debt. She was utterly filled with despair. She had always done it right. She went to church. She paid her taxes. She had been available to her husband but she was always unable to completely win his heart. When he finally left, her soul was flattened. She was filled with grief at the life she should have had.

James was a man full of life in his youth. He was the captain of the football team in high school. He lettered in three sports in college. He graduated at the top of his class, married a beautiful outgoing woman, landed a great job, and had his first child well before the age of twenty seven. By all accounts the future was bright and there was nothing that he could not accomplish. That was before cancer destroyed the muscle he had built on his body and robbed his soul of strength. James mourned the life he could have had.

Sandy and James are examples of the people we encounter who are in desperate need of the comfort which only Christ can bring. He most often brings it to them through us. The Scriptures offer more hope than they do answers to people in the midst of these monumental trials. This is not to say that the Bible does not have answers. It does. However, the greatest answer of God to a hurting and crushed soul often comes in the form of one who would simply mourn with those who mourn. Being present at a bedside, restaurant table for coffee, or even listening on the phone brings far more comfort than failed attempts to answer questions to which only God knows the full answer.

Whether it is a penitent heart, crushed by the weight of realization of the ugliness of its own sin or the broken heart with the unfair realities this life brings, blessed are those who mourn when they are comforted by the hand of Christ moving through us. When we are yielded to Christ we become the instrument of God's healing grace. When we are bound more by the love of God than the fear of reaching out, the Lord is able to use us to bring comfort to those who mourn. We are all pilgrims on this journey. How will we make it to our ultimate destination if we travel side by side as though we were alone?

Delilah is a wonderful woman of God. She prays regularly. She studies the Bible with great frequency. She and her husband even attend Bible seminars and are well read in the finest modern theological works. One morning in a Bible Study that I was teaching we began to talk about the personal nature of sin. There is no such thing as impersonal sin. It is not a mysterious force in the universe. It is the concrete actions committed in word and deed by humans acting according to their own motives. Choking back tears she explained how desperately sorrowful for her own sin that she was.

She was not speaking of a specific thing she had done last Tuesday while at the grocery store. She had conceived generally of how ugly sin, her personal sin, is comparison to the sweeping holiness of God. The realization of how ugly her sin is when contrasted with the beauty of God's perfection had grieved her heart so severely that she struggled under the weight of it. I was and remain entirely sympathetic to her plight. However, I did not try to erase her sorrow with a poetic exposition or flowery words.

I encouraged her the same way I shall seek to encourage you now. When we grieve for sin, we open the doorway to peace with God. Our hearts are never nearer to the heart of God than when we realize our own inadequacy and it drives us to total dependence upon God for forgiveness, mercy, and grace. Some are driven to shame and turn from God. This is not the way! Realization of our sinful state is the necessary precursor to casting our cares and burdens completely upon God.

It is tragic that the general tendency in the modern church is to redefine or simply neglect to teach about sin. When we avoid the topic of sin, we become spiritually like the man we discussed earlier who ignores a serious infection which eventually leads to his demise. We should glory in the fact that God has given us the privilege to know that we are sinful. Without the proper diagnosis no disease can find its cure! Sin treated becomes a bridge to freedom. Sin untreated, ignored, or redefined is the cancer that rots men's souls.

It is good to mourn our own sin. It is the corrupt fruit of human arrogance to treat as trite the ugliness of human corruption. Sin assaults God's perfect love for us. Sin is any act of the human will which seeks its own glory to the exclusion and subversion of the glory of God. Sin does not originate with God. There are instances where God uses temptation to sin to test and purify believers. Mourning one's sin may be, and often is, used by God to draw men to the love of Christ initially. The Scriptures bear witness to this and our experience of reality attests to it.

Sin does not originate with God. "When tempted, no one should say, 'God is tempting me.' For God cannot be tempted by evil, nor does he tempt anyone; but each one is tempted when, by his own evil desire, he is dragged away and enticed" (James 1:13-14). He did not create us to sin. Our fallenness is a reality that God, in His sovereignty foreknew and allowed; not caused. God is not the author of evil. He is righteous in judging mankind because of our sin.

Praise the God of all mercy and grace! In Jesus Christ He has judged sin and offered redemption. Praise God that He judges His children not according to the worthlessness of our evil, selfish, and corrupt works but in accordance with Christ's worth alone! By faith alone! By grace alone! As it has been revealed in the Scriptures alone! To His glory alone!

Sin does not originate with God. How tragic it is that so many believers see trials and temptations as flowing from the hand of God. We live in a fallen world where temptation and sin abound. We are fallen from the state of God's intended perfection and temptation and sin about within us. We are tempted from without, in our day, by a culture which has murdered common decency and traded the love of the truth for the love of a great trove and myriad of lies. Our ears and eyes are bombarded and our minds are assaulted with profanity, pornography, and all manner of indecency. We are tempted from all sides.

That temptation triggers the sinful nature which lives inside of all of us and we sin. The temptation comes from an outside source but the choice to sin or not to sin is solely with us. We know what is right and we deny it. We know innately that what we are about to do dishonors God, in many cases someone else, and always, ourselves, and yet time and again we choose poorly. Sin dishonors God because He is worthy of our obedience and yet we do not give it to Him. God has poured out the most radical grace, the most exuberant mercy, and yet we mock it in our near constant abandonment of His will in our lives.

It is not enough simply to deny ourselves the most carnal of sins. The Bible knows nothing of the carnal and the venial sins. Sin is sin because by its very nature it obscures the beauty, worth, and glory of God! There is no scale of acceptable, moderate, and terrible sins. Sin is not defined by its comparison with other sins. Sin is evil not because of the inherent manner of the action being committed. It is evil because any action which emanates from our corrupt hearts which is contrary to God's will and perfect love robs our loving Heavenly Father of the dignity, honor, and praise which is due to His holy name.

In other words, this matter of temptation and sin is not a legalistic matter of keeping a rigidly ordered moral and ethical life. While morals and ethics matter greatly, the greater matter is demeaning the glory and worth of God! Why do I strive to grow in the depth of honor which I give to my loving wife Christina? It is because I love her of course! God has loved us in a manner so reckless, in a fashion so unrelenting, that the only appropriate response is to mourn our sin and allow that mourning to drive us, not to guilt-laden obedience, but to radical repentance for the sake of His worth, out of the depth of our love for Him!

His glory extends from the highest of highs to the lowest of lows. He is worthy of adoration and obedience! Sin emanates from our evil desires. They are stronger than our ability to withstand them because we have fed them more than our love for God. We are not weak in our ability to withstand temptation because of our lack of knowledge of right and wrong. Even those who are far from the knowledge of God and His Church know innately what is wrong. It is written on the fabric of our very souls.

We are weak in our ability to withstand temptation because we are anorexic in our love for God. Fall in love with Jesus and watch the evil things of this life fade away into the mist of insignificance. Allow Christ to so fill your vision that you see everything through the lens of His beauty, redeeming the world for His glory! Fix your gaze so squarely upon Christ and His love, His worth, His beauty, that the rest of the world fades away into the mist of all things unimportant. This world is a vapor which is passing away. Christ's love alone remains forever!

Be so consumed by the mercy of God that His glory becomes the central motivation in your life and watch your power to resist temptation grow exponentially. It is not our strength but His love which empowers and enables us to avoid temptation. Penitence, that is mourning one's own sin, is a matter of the heart's attitude. Being penitent is having a sense of one's own need for the forgiveness of God because of one's own sin and shortcomings. Penitence, as with humility, is about poverty of the spirit; an attitude of sorrow over having denigrated the beauty of the One who loved us so radically that He didn't spare His own Son at the Cross.

Where pride destroys us, humility leads us to our knees in an attitude of penitent petition to God to forgive us our sins, to restore unto us the joy of our salvation, and to seal us with the presence of the Holy Spirit within us. Only the penitent man or woman will find their way to the place of absolute necessity for receiving the forgiveness, the grace, and the mercy of which they are in absolute need. When we bemoan our own sin, and indeed the ugliness of the human condition all around, we are never closer to the heart of God.

A penitent heart rightly leads us to a place of repentance. The condition of our soul will always have a practical outworking. A pride-filled heart will always lead to actions of a prideful nature. A heart filled with a sense of entitlement will always lead to a lack of appreciation. Just as faith must precede godly action, so whatever is inside of a person must find a way to express itself. No gluttonous and unattended dog will long allow the aroma of a freshly cooked carcass to go unattended by his lips and teeth. What is in our hearts will always express itself.

It is unfortunate that many Christians have replaced a lifestyle of repentance, a heart of genuine penitence, for an assumption of the necessity of shame. How many of us live under the burden of a nagging inner voice which constantly tells us, "you're not good enough, you don't measure up, and you are a failure"? Certainly there are times when all of us face situations in our lives, challenges and struggles that seem to be more than we can face. That is not so much what I am talking about here. All of us will have times of self-doubt where we need to learn to depend on God in ever increasing ways.

What I am talking about is the person consumed by shame from what someone else has done to them, personal past failures, or a person who, because of one or both of those things, is convinced not just that they are likely to fail in whatever they do, but is convinced that they will fail because they are a failure. Guilt is the right understanding that my sin places me necessarily in a place of responsibility to account for it in the light of the holiness and perfection of God. We all stand guilty before God for the sins that we have committed against other people in our lives and even the ways in which we have responded to the sins that others have committed against us. We are all guilty of sin but we are all equally forgiven of that sin by simple faith in Jesus Christ.

The Holy Spirit convicts us of sin and it is right that we should have a sense of guilt over the sin that we have committed. Shame, however, is counterfeit guilt. The shame that keeps us from knowing the completeness of the grace and love of God is a form of idolatry. God has forgiven the sins of those who have received Christ by faith. If He has judged sin in the terrible violence of the Cross, why do we make an idol of our own sin as though that judgment was not enough? God alone is judge. Judge not yourself.

Guilt leads us to our knees in repentance where we find forgiveness. Shame leads us only further into the depths of hiding from God. Guilt is the right recognition of sin while shame is the burden of the heart that never learns to live under, to reside in, and to be cleansed by, the superabundant grace of God. That grace is manifested in Jesus Christ and it is available as the result of the superabundant grace of God. It is accessible by faith, not by the pain that constant self-judgment and shame bring.

Guilt is good. It leads to repentance and freedom. Shame, that overbearing self-condemnation which many cast upon themselves, is the enemy of freedom. When we are bound by shame, we become the tyrannical jailor of our own souls! Celebrate guilt! It is the pathway to freedom from sin. Run quickly and feverishly from shame and self-condemnation into the arms of Christ where freedom awaits! Guilt is good because it is not only an emotional state. Guilt is the positional reality of the entire human race before a completely holy and just God.

Romans 3:23 says that "all have sinned and fall short of the glory of God." In the following verse, it goes on to say that we "are justified freely by his grace through the redemption that came by Christ Jesus" (Romans 3:24). Guilt of sin is propositional truth but shame is a denial of the redemption that has come freely in Christ. At the Cross, Jesus traded His glory for our guilt so that we might receive His glory in trade for the filthy rags of our sin! Child of God, you are a new creation. You are free! You are alive in Jesus Christ and no longer dead in sin, enslaved to this world and its cruel taskmaster – Satan and his chief agent, temptation.

Where shame enslaves, guilt, when brought before the throne of grace, destroys the shackles of the consequence and burden of sin. Dear friend, if we are to enjoy all that God has for us in this life we must embrace the heart's attitude of penitence. Rather than shame, we must respond rightly to our guilt by bringing it to the throne of mercy in repentance and embracing the grace that has been poured out to each one of us! We were not meant to wear shackles of lowliness or be enslaved by memories of past failures or what is in many cases, only the perception of past failures.

The forgiveness of sin is not based on our ability but His grace. Our mourning in this life shall one day be completely comforted when we see Him face to face. Until then we have the power of the very presence of God in our lives showering us with forgiveness, enabling us to let go of pride and shame as we embrace humility and grace! Fall in love with Christ and find in His arms the love of one who knows all of your shortcomings, all of your failures, all of your regrets, and yet smiles warmly and says, "Child, thou art loved with a love that knows no end, no boundary."

Chapter 3

"Blessed are the meek, for they will inherit the earth."
(Matthew 5:5)

It occurs to me that in the modern church culture most Christian churches fall on one or the other ends of a spectrum. On the one end of this spectrum there are those churches that, in an effort to be relevant to the culture, have made so much peace with the trends and shifting sands of society that they are practically indistinguishable from the culture. Western culture is very much like the sand dunes which lie just west of Yuma, Arizona. When I lived in that city I saw a picture of the dunes from several decades before and they were several miles away from where they are now.

On this end of the spectrum there is precious little difference between the gospel that is preached and the motivation speech which is pumped out of auditoriums during sales rallies, corporate training seminars, or get rich quick conferences. The church of Jesus Christ is called to be the constant in society just as God is unchanging and constant in the universe. Methods may change but our message is supposed to remain the unadulterated message of repentance by faith and salvation by grace.

I fear that the message being pumped out of much the body of Christ today is one of earthly prosperity by the seed of faith and salvation by works. Sure, most do not teach salvation by works overtly but what is the underlying message when the work of praying just the right prayer at the end of a worship service or telecast leads to salvation? What is being taught when God's glory is replaced as central in the lives of believers with our personal happiness? Christ did die on the Cross to make men free but He did this to glorify the Father.

The ultimate aim of all of God's activities is not my happiness but His glory. I receive joy along the way as I enter into participation with God's plan of redemption for the world and salvation for my life. I praise Him because of His worth and celebrate His goodness. I do not praise Him in order to get His goodness in my life. A simple honest open-eyed appraisal of much of what passes for Christian faith today bears out that many Christians are much more interested in what God can do for them in the here and now than they are with what God requires from them today.

This may sound like a harsh, overly critical appraisal of modern church culture. Consider seriously the reality of the modern church for just a moment and I think you will likely agree. Are we any less consumer minded than the culture? Who are our celebrities? Are they people like the elderly woman who loves the Lord desperately, spending hours on her knees crying out to God to save her wayward grandchild and unbelieving children? Are they the local pastor who serves his small parish faithfully though he is terribly underpaid and his wife is stricken with cancer?

These saintly people are not the thing of our modern celebrity Christian culture! It is an embarrassment to the pure Gospel of Jesus Christ that we are even as celebrity-driven as the culture. The fact that we celebrate the most charming, successful, bright smiled, wealthy, and prominent television preachers is a sad commentary on what our hearts crave. Rather than serving the world meekly, humbly, in the love and power of Christ, we are drawn like moths to the flame of worldly success and easy ego-petting preaching.

We are called to be meek, humble, servants of the world. Jesus suffered and died on our behalf. Are we called to do anything less for the world? Our calling is to receive His overwhelming love and to share in it by passing it on to others. The greatest way to experience the love of Christ is to share it with others. If we long for blessings then we must redefine our standards of what a blessing is according to God's standard not our own. I grew up in a family of low financial means. I know the struggle of not fitting into the culture due to a lack of the right brand of shoes in elementary and middle school. I also know what it is like to live in the modern church family where we are so filled with material blessings and so spiritually poor.

Blessed are the meek, not the rich. I once heard it said that the greatest advantage that the rich have over the poor is not their material wealth. It is the knowledge that what they already have, that material wealth, never brings true happiness. The personal lives of the wealthy are just as tangled as the personal lives of everyone else. Indeed, when the economy recently collapsed, it probably had a more immediately earth-shattering effect on the very rich than the very poor. If you have nothing to lose, all can be taken and it matters very little.

The trouble is that we have too much to lose. Jesus said "What good is it for a man to gain the whole world, yet forfeit his soul?" (Mark 8:36). The point that I making is not that material wealth is inherently evil. Forbid that any should believe the provision of God to be evil. The point here is the focus of our minds and the affection of our hearts. Blessed are the meek for they have set aside self for the glory of God. Blessed are the meek for they have used their wealth to bring glory to God.

For many others, the Gospel has become little more than a vehicle of good will. Though well-intentioned, the redefined Gospel as a means of social moral change is little more than a parody of the true Gospel. Jesus preached repentance and faith. He said that the Kingdom of God is at hand and we must turn from sin, from seeking to exalt self, and instead turn to a lifestyle of discipleship. We are to become like Christ through the transforming power of Christ's love dwelling in us.

Christianity is about so much more than easy believism and feeling better about oneself. Of course there is joy and peace in

39

knowing Christ and in being known by God. There is great joy that comes through the presence of the Holy Spirit in the life of the believer. The true and lasting joy of the believer is vastly different from what is being pumped out of so many churches today. We have traded the joy of salvation for the promise of earthly prosperity. We have sold our birthright of eternal inheritance for the pottage of temporal, fleeting happiness.

Lasting peace comes from finding peace with God through identifying ourselves with the sacrifice of Jesus! "I have been crucified with Christ and I no longer live, but Christ lives in me. The life I live in the body, I live by faith in the Son of God, who loved me and gave himself for me." (Galatians 2:20). This life is not primarily about this life! We have repeatedly forgotten that to know Christ in His suffering is of more worth than all of the wealth and prosperity that this world can give.

Hope, security, and joy comes from being awakened to the reality of the assurance of Christ residing in one's very being! Happiness, lasting and complete happiness, comes from discovering the truth that no matter what we may find in this life, we are found in Christ! Pure delight for the believer is that no matter what state we find ourselves to be in, as we pass along this pilgrimage we are passing through guided, covered, filled, and consumed by the love of Jesus Christ. When our focus is on finding peace we will never find it. When our focus is on finding Christ we will receive all of the beauty that His love brings with it.

I know what you may be thinking. This fellow plainly dropped out or was kicked out of the contemporary-school-for-prosperity-motivational-feel-good-preaching! Indeed. I don't think I ever even applied to that school, and if I had, surely they would have rejected my application. Knowing Christ has precious little to do with gain in this life. The passing material beauty of this world is a snare which entangles many and snuffs out the pure life of Christ in many more. Heavenly meekness, not earthly glory is the pilgrim path to true prosperity. Knowing Christ is the greatest treasure of this life. This life is not about this life and I am not the center of the universe.

To be sure, the Gospel message of repentance and salvation according to the grace of God and the gift of faith is a positive message but not because it is about us. It is because at its heart it is about the glorification of God in us and that, my dear friends, has the ability to change our heart. If you seek freedom from anxiety, seek Christ and watch His love crush your anxiety. If you seek hope, seek Christ and find in Him the hope of eternity and the reality of His love conquering all of your fears!

I am reminded of the zeal and enthusiasm of the average contestant on the popular television show "Deal or No Deal!" My wife and I are fascinated with people's reactions and attitudes on the show. It is a real microcosm of the human condition in our culture. If you have not seen the show, the contestant is given one of several briefcases and then completely at random picks briefcases to discard. The briefcases contain dollar amounts ranging from one dollar to the ultimate million dollar prize. After every few cases, the "banker" makes an offer to the contestant. He can accept this offer or deny it.

The offer gets higher or lower based on the likelihood that a high dollar case is the one in possession of the contestant. As the drama unfolds the contestant and their family or friends will grow excited. They will cry, laugh, and often go through the full gamut of human emotions. Seldom does a contestant on the show leave with more than a tenth of the grand prize but many win much more than that. For the promise of temporal earthly wealth people will empty their body of hydration, crying rivers of tears. They will exhaust themselves with shouts of exuberance.

Each Sunday morning the doors of our churches open and the throngs come in. The preacher expounds on the wonder of eternal grace, the everlasting promise of the streets of heaven covered in gold, and in the reality of the love of our crucified and risen Savior descending to take up residence in our very hearts. Seldom is a tear shed. Rarely does a cry of joy echo from the ceiling. Precious saints of God, we don't need a counterfeit gospel fashioned after the pride and prosperity of this world when we have the awe striking wonder of the Gospel of the irresistible love of God crashing over us!

The uplifting thing about the Christian message is that when Christ was lifted up on Calvary a means for my being reconciled completely with the God, who loves us so recklessly as to send His own Son, was secured! The encouraging thing about the Christian message is that in Christ we have been granted access to an encouragement far greater than that offered by any motivational speaker. Our hearts are encouraged by the very presence of Christ within us. The positivity of the Christian message is namely that our redeemer lives. And because He lives, you and I live in Him now and for all eternity.

There are still other believers that are so adamant about keeping the Gospel message pure that they see themselves as somehow at war with the world. These folks, while preaching the message of salvation by grace according to faith, have made the Kingdom of God in the image of the kingdoms of the world. While they are well-intentioned, they have missed the mark of the pure Gospel message. It is found plainly in the words of Christ in the Sermon on the Mount. All of the words of the beatitudes flow together. Each of the principals leads to the next principal in an orderly fashion.

The general theme in the beatitudes is the way of the spiritual pilgrimage of this life. The way of Jesus is the way of the spiritual pilgrim. We are strangers in this world and we should look radically different from it. Humility places us in the position to exalt God in our lives. Penitence is the way of mourning over one's sins as we see God for who He is in the universe. Now, as we come to the principle of meekness we find that Jesus is not telling us to be weak but rather but to be strong in Him. Jesus is not saying that we ought to be timid and fearful. In II Timothy 1:7 the Bible says,

"For God did not give us a spirit of timidity, but a spirit of power, of love and of self-discipline."

Meekness has nothing to do with being small and insignificant. It is has everything to do with being yielded to His power, His will, and His direction in our lives. We are strong in His strength. We are yielded to His power. We are able to stand strong in the power of His might. When we yield only to our own preferences, we are truly weak. We are like the mouse who brazenly takes the cheese from the trap.

He is conceited with his ability and so singly concerned with his prize that his ego leads him to his death. He dies with his little mouse hands still clinging to the cheese. Are we any different when we take control of our lives? We follow the lure of pleasure only to later find ourselves addicted to it and ruled by its grip. We follow the lure of wealth only to find that our constant pursuit of career, material gain, and prestige has caused us to alienate all of the people who really matter in our lives.

In these first three beatitudes, these steps along the pilgrim's path, we see that each of them in their own way is pointing away from self and unto God, even as they are pointing away from pride unto humility, penitence, and meekness. To be yielded to the will of God means that we seek after His glory rather than our own glory. It means that rather than resting in our strength we will rest in His. Ultimately, being yielded to the will of God means that we will choose to operate within whatever circumstances we find ourselves in a way that reflects the His love and as we do we will find that our loosened grip on this life is replaced by a tightened grip on our life by our Heavenly Father.

It is incredibly difficult for us to understand what it means when Jesus says that the meek will inherit the earth. We are programmed for prosperity not humility. The story is told of the paralytic man who was wheeled down the aisle and placed near the altar at an evangelistic meeting. As the service began the choir director saw him and said, "What is your favorite hymn?" Without delay he answered, "Count Your Blessings!" He didn't cry out in complaint for his status in life. He cried out with humility and adoration at the goodness and glory of God.

Our submissiveness, how completely we are yielded to God, dictates the level of satisfaction that we will have in this life. "Blessed are the meek: for they shall inherit the earth" (Matthew 5:5). The paralytic man in this story is worthy of a far greater inheritance than many a millionaire. Meekness is power. It is the power to be satisfied with what God gives us, no matter what that may be. Meekness brings the power not merely to endure but to enjoy each day to the fullest and to use it for His purpose.

Blessed are the meek for in the trials of this life they understand that it not their will but God's that is to be done. They know that it is not their glory which is to be sought but God's glory alone which is central. What greater joy can any man or woman have than that of being a humble vessel of God's grace? No greater treasure exists in the entire universe than that of the meek, who shall inherit not merely a crown of gold or a pieces of silver, but the earth!

But you say, "How do I do it?" That is a fair question. How do we become people who are more completely yielded to the will of God than self-will? The answer is that we must learn to trust Christ and to follow His example. I understand that may sound like overstated simplicity. "So, the preacher says to be like Jesus. Great! How do I do that?" God's will in our life is that we would absolutely learn to follow Jesus example of meekness. We make it more complicated. We build the task of following Jesus to impossible loftiness. Following Jesus is not painless but it is simple. A straightforward humble attitude of the heart is what meekness is all about.

Jesus said at the time of His crucifixion that He could have called upon legions of angels to rescue Him. He had and still has all of the power of God at His disposal. Yet He exercised great meekness and submission to the will of the Father. He is our chief example. He is the foundation of our faith. In the Garden of Gethsemane, on the eve of the crucifixion, Jesus prayed, "Father, if you are willing, take this cup from me; yet not my will, but yours be done" (Luke 22:42). No matter what life brings along our path, our ultimate joy is always found in yielding ourselves to His perfect will.

Even when the way is hard, even when we can't understand the reason for the suffering, the temptation, or the heartache that we face, it is in trusting God's will completely that we find the strength we need. Not my will but His. Not my glory but His. Not my stubborn pride but His perfect will through humble obedience and meek devotion to His voice in my life. That means that like Jesus in the Garden of Gethsemane we see the encroaching and present trial for what it is. We don't hide from it. We face it yielded to God's will.

I have been to the Garden of Gethsemane. On my first trip to the Holy Land I went there with a tour group of other pastors. What a wonderful experience it was to walk in that grove ancient olive trees nestled beneath the Temple Mount. When I was there I noticed that someone had left a small hand-crafted wooden cross leaning against an ancient olive tree. The olive tree has long represented life to the Jewish people. The Cross of Christ, of course, represents death and new life.

In the garden, on the eve of the crucifixion, we see Jesus fully engulfed in the unending pain and humiliation of the Cross. He was overwhelmed with the sorrow He would soon endure. In the face of such grief He offered His agony to the Father, seeking not His own will to be done, not what was the most immediately comfortable to Him, but that which would please the Father and bring about the ultimate good for humanity. Meek is not synonymous with feeble. Meekness is not the pathetic attempt to spiritualize frailty! Meekness is the spiritual virtue of those who seek the Lord's power to be demonstrated through their submission to the Lord's will.

True power is acquired by the meek in their obedience to the will of Almighty God! Jesus conquered sin and death through obedience to the Father's will on the Cross. Through the violence of the Cross, the power of the grace of God was manifest fully in salvation. The abundant mercy of God was forged on the anvil of Golgotha's cruelty. Speaking of Jesus growing ministry and the decline of his own, John the Baptist said that "He must become greater; I must become less" (John 3:30).

The same is true for us. Every Christian wants more of God in their lives and this is the way to achieving that goal. In a very real sense to achieve the goal of knowing God, we must abandon that goal altogether. We can reach out to heaven in our strength for the rest of our lives and never reach high enough. Knowing the power of God is not about us reaching out for Him. The strength of God is attained as we yield the entirety of our lives to Him. We must be yielded to God as a patient under anesthesia is yielded to the surgeon.

I find such delight in being a father. I look forward to the big days of weddings, graduations, and the like to be sure but I relish the joys of their childhood. My youngest son, Ephram, sleeps on the bottom bunk in the "Mickey Mouse Room" that he shares with his older brother Sebastian. Recently two-year-old Ephram, who has only recently began to attempt such feats as climbing ladders, decided that he was going to climb up to Sebastian's top bunk. Normally he is able to climb to the top but this time, in his half-awake, overly-sleepy state, he got his foot tangled in the ladder and began to fall. Of course, I grabbed him before he could fall but he was scared. He began to whimper a bit and let out a halfhearted, tired cry.

I lifted him to the top where he wanted to go. I held him under his little arms and I looked directly into his bright eyes and said, "Ephram, Daddy won't let you fall. Daddy is right here!" He smiled through his mild tears and halfhearted sobs and said 'O-o-o-tay.'" In Mark 10:15 Jesus says, "I tell you the truth, anyone who will not

receive the kingdom of God like a little child will never enter it."
We often make dependence upon God a great deal more
complicated than it needs to be.

Jesus says that the kingdom is received with the heart of a child
crying out "Daddy, Abba, don't let me fall. Abba, be near!" The
kingdom of God is found wherever God exercises perfect
dominion. God's reign in Heaven is perfect but in the earth there
remains rebellion, hatred, injustice, and sin. While God is perfectly
sovereign over His creation, that creation has used the freedom
granted to it to rebel against His grace, love, and will. In meekness,
obedience, submissiveness, abandonment to the providence of
God, we look unto the author and finisher of our faith, setting
aside our own feeble power for His immeasurable and never-ending
strength!

Chapter 4

"Blessed are those who hunger and thirst for righteousness, for they will be filled." (Matthew 5:6)

What tragedy and glory are mingled in the image of the crown of thorns! The truly astonishing thing is that while its shame belonged to me, Christ bore the shame in my place. The glory that was His alone, He gave to me in its place. I deserved to wear that crown. I deserved to feel the thrust of the thorns. I deserved to feel the warm trickle of blood upon my brow. I deserved the pain. He took my crown of thorns and gave to me His crown of life. There is healing for us available in His broken hands.

The Bible says that after Jesus had hung on the Cross for some time, "… knowing that all was now completed, and so that the Scripture would be fulfilled, Jesus said, "I am thirsty" (John 19:28). Some people standing nearby gave him sour wine vinegar to drink. The one who offers the pure water of life was given sour wine to drink. In the gospel of John 4:14 Jesus says, "But whoever drinks of the water that I will give him will never be thirsty again. The water that I will give him will become in him a spring of water welling up to eternal life."

Jesus death on the Cross was payment for sin. God is like a righteous judge who must account for our wrongdoing. He is also a merciful and loving God. He reconciled justice and mercy by pardoning our sin through the sacrifice of His own Son. Jesus death on the Cross was the substitutionary atonement foreshadowed in the ancient rites of Old Testament Israel. Jesus did not die unwillingly at the hands of the Romans, following the taunting of the Jewish leaders. Jesus died to fulfill the promise of a substitution to satisfy the holiness of God. His death was a payment for our sin, a substitution on our behalf to satisfy the wrath of God incurred by sin so that God might justly display His radical mercy and grace! It was also a globally public display for all generations to see the degree to which we need a savior. In other words, Jesus hung on Calvary's cruel Cross to highlight our need for His love.

When the God of all grace and glory sent perfect beauty into this world, we hung it on a tree. God demonstrated His own love for us in that "while were yet sinners Christ died for us" (Romans 5:8). The God of creation sent us a sort of living telegram, His word made flesh, and we murdered it! We pierced its hands, feet, and side, and thrust a crown of thorns upon its head. The fact of the Cross both provides for our forgiveness and highlights our need for it. We are all like the careless child who catches a marvelous butterfly only to crush it in our clumsy little hands.

What's worse is that Jesus was not crushed by mistake. This sinful world, of which we are a part, always destroys what is most beautiful. The mysterious beauty of God's love for us is that when the beautiful Rose of Sharon, Christ, was trampled, His death became the fragrance of life! When we are in Christ we become likewise, the fragrance of life in a world sickened by the stench of its own decay. Jesus says "Blessed are those who hunger and thirst for righteousness, for they will be filled" (Matthew 5:6).

What does it mean to hunger and thirst for righteousness? What does it mean to be filled? I lived for four years in the Arizona desert. I was stationed there at the Marine Corps Air Station in Yuma from 1999 until 2003 when I was discharged. I love the desert. I have spent many hours walking desert trails with little more than my camera in my hand and a supply of water on my back. I have walked miles of those desert hills and I know how parched one can become in a very short time in the desert heat.

One Sunday afternoon while I was making my way from a trip in the desert to a local nursing home to preach, I noticed a man walking a bike along the road. The temperature that day was well above one hundred degrees. He looked as though he was on the verge of collapse. He was covered in sweat. His clothes were faded and tattered. I pulled off of the road just ahead of him and waited for a few moments until he was near. I had just purchased two brand new ice cold plastic bottles of water. I stepped out of my dusty Ford Bronco and offered him a ride and a frosty bottle of water. He refused both.

I was somewhat dumfounded. To be honest I assumed that he was either a little bit delirious from the heat or just out of his mind. Why on earth would anyone rather walk thirsty in the heat than ride comfortably and sip some cold water? I have since that time wondered if perhaps he was unsure of my intentions. Perhaps he was just being careful. Perhaps human nature is such that often we are all like that man. We walk alone in the desert of spiritual blindness and even when we are offered the refreshing water that our souls seek, we are too foolish to rinse the dust from our eyes and drink.

In John 6:35 Jesus says "I am the bread of life. He who comes to me will never go hungry, and he who believes in me will never be thirsty." A hunger for righteousness is the longing of our souls to be reconciled with God. It is a deep spiritual yearning to commune with God. This longing is not reserved for the mystic or the monk. It is innate to all of us. Those who would be filled are not only scholars and theologians. Indeed, it has been my experience that it is the simple, the humble, the meek, who are most likely to be filled and truly satisfied by the filling that faith brings.

Adeline was a precious and saintly woman. At more than ninety years old she would recount stories from her past with amazing accuracy. Her mind was lucid and her soul alive. There was one theme which always connected Adeline's tales of the past – a simple love for God and a genuine love for people. This was one theme because I am convinced that her love for God animated her love for people. Hers was an uncomplicated faith. Her soul had been

51

filled with the deep satisfaction that comes with simply receiving the free offer of living water which Christ gives.

In all of the beatitudes Jesus is contrasting the wisdom of the world with the wisdom of God. He is spelling out in no uncertain terms what it means to be a citizen of the Kingdom. That is how followers of Jesus Christ are called to live. We are called paradoxically, somewhat illogically, to the abundant blessing which comes from hungering and thirsting and being filled. Blessed are those who hunger and thirst because in their longing they will hear the voice of God and respond. Blessed are those who are filled because as their being is filled, they will know the overwhelming beauty of the filling of His love and mercy!

Only someone who is truly hungry will seek nourishment. Hunger and thirst for God is a blessing because as a result of our thirst we will accept the offer of living water. Apart from having some strange disorder, every human being recognizes the need to eat and drink for physical sustenance. Why is it that so many ignore or neglect their spiritual hunger until they become like the starving child in a third world country who, after months of malnutrition, loses his appetite? Though they are wasting away spiritually, they no longer hunger or thirst.

We have become physical gluttons and spiritual anorexics. We feed our natural carnal appetites so much that they are out of control and we starve our spirits to such an extent that they are wasting away. Physically we are bloated. Spiritually we are mere skeletal remnants of what God has intended us to be. God created humanity to live in relationship with Him. Intrinsic in our very composition is a bent toward knowing God, toward being spiritually hungry and thirsty.

The terrible folly of our day is a perverted hunger and thirst. We were created to worship God, to hunger for His righteousness, yet we feed our appetites with lesser foods, lesser gods.

When humanity fell into sin our nature was corrupted by the power of rebellion and yet not fully destroyed. Every man, woman, and child on this planet is worshiping something, though it likely is not what that they were created to worship. There are those who have exchanged the pure worship of God for a restatement of God into their own image. These, though having a form of religious devotion, have cast aside the power and majesty of the pure worship of the God of the ages who has revealed Himself in the Bible. To these folks God is little more than a familiar and comforting concept from childhood.

There are those who have abandoned God outright. They have declared not His will be done but theirs! Crying out with every fiber of their being, if not with every action and decision of their life, "I am the master of my own destiny. In my own wisdom, strength, and knowledge I will place my trust!" For this increasing segment of our population the Gospel message is an affront to their own way and it is for that central reason that it and the God of which it speaks are rejected. As the Apostle Paul writes in Romans 1:25-26, "They exchanged the truth of God for a lie, and worshiped and served created things rather than the Creator – who is forever praised... Because of this, God gave them over to shameful lusts."

We see the fulfillment of this in our very day and the continuation of it from the days of old. Whenever and wherever men have abandoned, denied, or rejected the only true and living God, in spite of His absence, something has been worshiped. Just as man's physical being is unsustainable without nourishment, just as man's body is naturally bent to hunger and thirst for the physical nourishment of bread and water, so too man's natural state is to live in an attitude of worship. Be a person pagan, Christian, Buddhist, modern naturalist, or outright atheist, rest assured, there is yet to be a person born who does not live out the days of their life worshiping something.

It is precisely our hunger and thirst for things other than God which lead us into temptation and sin. Blessed are those who hunger and thirst for righteousness because a hunger for God will compel each of us to have our eyes so set upon Christ and His glory and worth that we will avoid temptation and sin simply because we are so much more concerned with resting in and sharing the love of God. When Jesus becomes the focus of our vision, the rest of this world fades away until Christ is at the heart of all that we are.

When Christ is the thing for which we hunger, we will make Him known in our business practices. When Christ is that for which we thirst, His love will flood our souls as though it were the ocean filling a thimble. It will spill out all round us! When our hearts hunger for wealth, we will dishonor the worth of God. When our hearts thirst for power, we will deny the providential authority of God in our lives. Sin is really a simple matter. It is the corrupt fruit of rebellious hearts who, rather than thirsting for the eternal joy of life with God, thirst for the passing fancy of pleasure in this fading world.

The question we must ask of ourselves is "For what do we hunger and thirst?" I have a nearly insatiable appetite for circus peanuts. If you have never heard of or tried these, you really should. Or perhaps not, should you share my addictive tendencies for sweets! They are a miracle of modern confections. They are a little orange candy that look like a peanut. Only, unlike their naturally grown namesake, they have the consistency of a marshmallow without being a marshmallow. They are sweet without being overwhelming. In short, they are great!

My love affair with circus peanuts is probably rooted as much in my life experience as it is rooted in their great texture and flavor. My maternal great-grandmother, whom we all affectionately called "Granny", used to give me these tasty treats as a little boy. Its amazing, isn't it, the way a certain flavor, a certain smell, or even a certain sound, can take us back to days gone by? I loved my granny deeply and I have been eating those circus peanuts all of my life. Our sinful appetites are just the same way. We have feasted on the things of the world, the sweet tasting but empty calories of sinful pleasure and selfish concerns for so long that our appetites long for those things, rather than the truth of God's word and the beauty of His love for us.

If we are to fulfill Jesus' admonition to hunger and thirst for God, if we are to feast on the eternally satisfying things of God, then we must retrain our appetites. That can only happen to the extent that we immerse ourselves in the truth of the Bible, the heart's worship of God, and become devoted followers of Jesus Christ. We shall never be deeply or eternally satisfied eating the candy upon which we have feasted for so long. Sin is like sugar. It tastes sweet but causes decay and leaves us empty and malnourished.

Dear friend, fall in love with Jesus and watch the evil things of this life fade away into the mist of insignificance. Allow Christ to so fill your vision that you see everything through the lens of His beauty, redeeming the world for His glory! Allow yourself to be so consumed by the mercy of God that His glory becomes the central motivation in your life. Your power to resist temptation, to live in victory, and to rest in God's peace grows exponentially. It is not our strength which makes us strong. It is a hunger for, and filling with, His love which enables us every step along the sacred journey of following Jesus through the arid places of this life!

In Matthew 6:24 Jesus says, "No one can serve two masters. Either he will hate the one and love the other, or he will be devoted to the one and despise the other. You cannot serve both God and Money." Though Jesus gives the example of money taking precedence in our lives over God, the same could be said of many things. You cannot serve both God and pride. You cannot serve both God and blind ambition. You cannot serve both God and any other thing because Jesus' point here is that at the very core of our nature we have been made to worship God and anything that takes the place of our affection for God is malnourishment. The nourishment which our soul hungers and thirsts for is the nourishment of Christ's very presence, the Holy Spirit of God residing in us.

The desperate trouble is that through anorexic spiritual living we have lost the sense of hunger that was hard wired into us from our very birth. It is an interesting thing that happens to people with eating disorders. After even a number of weeks and months of living with anorexia, a person's appetite begins to change. After long periods of going without food an anorexic person begins to crave food less and less. A physical change occurs in them as they abandon their natural desire for food. Anorexia is a terrible disease which afflicts many people in our narcissistic, vanity-driven culture.

It affects primarily women and, while the specific cause of anorexia is unknown, common factors can be easily discerned. It almost always involves a poor self image which is largely driven by a culture that worships false narrow standards of physical beauty. This plays out to the detriment of those who see themselves as unequally beautiful. Though many in our culture have abandoned the worship of God, they have not abandoned worship entirely. The worship of physical beauty, as defined arbitrarily by such standards as magazine covers, thrives. Temples built to the worship of self are not hard to find.

In John 15:5 Jesus says, "I am the vine; you are the branches. If a man remains in me and I in him, he will bear much fruit; apart from me you can do nothing." Contrary to the conception that each of us is the center of our own universe, our ultimate source of life and worth is Christ. The nourishment for which our souls hunger and thirst is the nourishment that is found in abandoning the worship of oneself in favor of the worship of God. Let us care for the body because the Bible says that it is the temple of the Holy Spirit. Let us care for the body to enable a long life of service the Lord, not in order to meet the arbitrary standards of beauty and self worship of our day. Ultimate worth comes directly from the source of all life.

It comes through an intimate connection with the vine which nourishes our souls; the worship of the one only True and Living God who offers the nourishment and satisfaction that we long for freely through His Son Jesus Christ! Today, if your soul is weary, come to the fountain of pure water that flows beneath the Cross of Jesus Christ. Today, if your soul is tired, abandon the yoke of slavery to self, self image, and self will. Pick up the yoke of Christ which is easy and light. Find the rest that your souls so desperately longs for!

In the book of Exodus is found the familiar account of the provision of God in the form of bread from Heaven for the Israelites after they fled Egypt and Pharaoh. In Exodus 16:31 it says, "The people of Israel called the bread manna. It was white like coriander seed and tasted like wafers made with honey." Just as the Lord provided for His people in the desert by sending them bread from heaven for the nourishment of their physical bodies, God has provided for us bread from Heaven for the nourishment of our very souls eternally.

In I Corinthians 10:1-4 the Apostle Paul writes, "For I do not want you to be ignorant of the fact, brothers, that our forefathers were all under the cloud and that they all passed through the sea. They were all baptized into Moses in the cloud and in the sea. They all ate the same spiritual food and drank the same spiritual drink; for they drank from the spiritual rock that accompanied them, and that rock was Christ." When our affection is set squarely upon Christ the thirsting of our souls will be quenched and our eternal hunger satisfied.

There is a place near where Christina and I used to live in Florida, called Wall Spring Park. When Sebastian was a baby and then very little and first beginning to walk, she and I would regularly take him there. We would often push him in the stroller around this beautiful pathway which had been built on a several acre area. On one side of the park there was a very nice playground. On another end of the park there were scenic outlooks which provided incredible views of the Gulf Coast.

There was even an elevated platform which could be climbed to see for miles around the Palm Harbor, Florida area. The park and pathways were centered though, around Wall Springs. This little pool of bubbling crystal clear water feeds an equally clear pond which makes its way eventually to a bayou which runs into the ocean. It is a wonderful place that we enjoyed very much. Life was obvious and visible in the clear water with fish of many varieties and Florida wildlife of all kinds abundant in the water of the spring.

There are pictures dotting the entire area of people being refreshed in the water in years past when there was a pool house built for recreation in the water prior to its becoming a natural sanctuary for the area wildlife. There is an abundant fountain, a spring, which flows freely with the water of eternal life, eternal nourishment, eternal refreshment, eternal peace and life! Speaking to the Samaritan woman at the well, Jesus said, "'Everyone who drinks this water will be thirsty again, but whoever drinks the water I give him will never thirst. Indeed, the water I give him will become in him a spring of water welling up to eternal life'" (John 4:13-14).

You and I have been created to worship God. It is as natural to the life of our spiritual being as eating and drinking is to the life of our natural bodies! We need to come to the fountain of living water – Jesus Christ – to receive the satisfaction for the thirst of our souls. We need only to set aside the worship of all peripheral things in favor of worshiping the only true and Living God who has given us life through Jesus Christ.

Chapter 5

"Blessed are the merciful, for they will be shown mercy."
(Matthew 5:7)

There are few things of human engineering which are more beautiful to watch than the marching of the Marine Corps Silent Drill Team. To see them move in perfect sync is astounding as they pivot on a dime, all in unison or in perfect order, as they loft their hand-polished, ten and one-half pound, M-1 Garand rifles, through the air and catch them; often throwing them to one another. With every step that is taken there is the smooth swooshing of their uniforms and the quick snap of their shoe heels as they come back together in seamless unison and the tight rap of their hands slapping the stock of their rifles.

As a Marine Corps photographer stationed at the Marine Corps Air Station Yuma, I had the privilege of documenting their winter training in the Arizona desert. I, and the other photographers with whom I worked, knew the sounds of the silent drill team very well. The Church Fathers, in their theology, expressed the sounds of the precision and snap of God's actions; they have passed down to us a great legacy of the stirring sounds of the wrath of God. Many Modern ears, however, have heard only the soft swooshing of God's favor, but have not listened for the rifle and the sharp click of the heel.

The beauty of the sovereign God of creation is understood most fully in the light of all that He is. He is not merely the God of delicate sentimentality. He is not the God who exists primarily to bring pleasure to this earthly existence. He is far greater than the all too common shallow platitudes of our empty praises. His heights are grander than the steepest mountains and His beauty far surpasses any of the wonders of this world which our eyes have beheld.

He is just and He loves. He is strong and He is also slow to anger, abundant in mercy. Kindness without justice is mere sentiment. Justice without mercy has no power to transform the stubborn heart of mankind. Barely does it even have the power to cause it to acquiesce, to submit. The cross is the only place where the portrait of God is in complete focus. God's justice and mercy come together in His love for sinners. God is neither vengeful nor is He filled with a light-hearted kind of sentimental love. He is just. He is righteous. He is holy. He loves. He is full of grace. God is truth tempered with mercy.

In the Church we often speak of grace. What of mercy? Are they exchangeable ideals? Are they but perhaps two sides of the same coin? Let us not mistake grace for mercy or mercy for grace. They are both equally important and distinct. Grace is how God has dealt with our sin. Mercy is how God deals with us. Grace is the act of God in granting sinful humanity a pardon from the penalty for sin. Mercy is God's love expressed to us even as we deal with the consequences of our own sin.

In other words, grace is the means by which Christ died to provide for us atonement and forgiveness for sins; mercy is Christ present with me, carrying me, holding me, assuring me, while I walk through the storms of this life. In Matthew 5:7 Jesus says, "Blessed are the merciful, for they will be shown mercy." If we are to walk full in the knowledge of His strength, His holiness, and His justice, we also must learn to reside in and rest in His grace, His forgiveness, and His mercy. Mercy is something to be experienced because mercy is grace's practical counterpart. Often we confuse the two as though they were the same. They are not.

Grace is the means of His presence with me. Mercy is the reality of His presence within me in the here and now circumstances of life. Grace is how God dealt with sin. Mercy is how He deals with me. Grace is defined as unmerited favor or unwarranted goodwill. Grace is the way that God relates to us in regard to our sin problem while mercy is the way God relates to me in the everyday problems of this life. It is according to God's abundant grace that our sins have been forgiven. It is according to His abundant mercy that I find the peace, hope, and strength to face the challenges of every day.

In Romans 5:17 the Apostles Paul writes, "For if, by the trespass of the one man, death reigned through that one man, how much more will those who receive God's abundant provision of grace and of the gift of righteousness reign in life through the one man, Jesus Christ." According to grace, sins are forgiven through faith in Jesus Christ. According to mercy, God deals with each one of us even in our imperfection, inadequacy, and insufficiency. Where we are weak, He is strong. Where there is a need, He provides it. Where we are crooked, He gently straightens us out.

In recent years I have begun to garden. My garden has grown from a collection of upside down hanging planters which I purchased after seeing a late night television commercial, to a few large raised beds and several tomato caged pots. One of the many things that has amazed me about gardening is the way that a plant naturally grows toward the light. When I start seeds on the back porch of our home, the little seedlings will bend every which way to grow toward the light. The plants do what we should always do as well. They abhor the darkness and face the light.

This bending to grow toward the light has made several of my seedlings lay over significantly when they are removed from the porch and planted in the garden in early spring. I have found that this is easy to combat. Since the plants always want to grow toward the light I have placed some of them in a more shaded area in such a way that they have to grow in the opposite direction to reach the fullest sunlight. Adjusting their position slightly makes them straighten out as they bend toward their source of life.

God deals similarly mercifully with His people. He mercifully moves us as we grow. He shapes us. He removes obstacles in our lives which block us from receiving the fullness of His light. According to the depth of His grace God has showered us with forgiveness in Jesus Christ. By simple faith we receive the gift of eternal life. The unwrapping of that gift is not a task reserved for Heaven. As we unpack our understanding of the vastness of His love for us, we discover that He is gently guiding us, mercifully transforming us.

In Matthew 5:7 it may appear as though Jesus is implying that only those who show mercy will receive it. To be sure, there is a principle that runs throughout the Scriptures in regard to sowing and reaping. If we plant seeds of mercy in the lives of those around us we will be more likely to reap a harvest of mercy from others. To be sure, what Jesus is telling us relates not only to our relationship with God but with other people. Perhaps you, like me have known someone in your life that was so unmerciful to others that no one , if given the chance, would likely show any mercy to them.

What of those who because of pain and disappointment, selfishness, or some other force, are unmerciful all the days of their lives? What of them, should they come to a place in their lives when they are no longer able to stand in their own strength and find themselves in the place of needing mercy, help, love from those around them? They find that their lack of compassion for others has caused them to be alone and without the very mercy that they so rarely shared with others. Now, in desperate need of mercy, there is none to be found.

What Jesus is telling us is that if we want to experience mercy from God we must be willing to share mercy with others. He is calling us into a way of life which is characterized by reciprocal mercy. The message of this passage is not that God only shows mercy to the merciful. He is saying that if we want to elicit mercy from others then we must show it to them. Even more, if we are to fully experience the mercy of God, then we must be willing vessels who not only receive mercy, but conduits who share mercy with others.

This is not only true of our personal spiritual lives. It is also true of our communal faith life. The church is supposed to be a healing place. I sometimes envision the local church that I pastor as having its walls covered with soft pads. This is not to imply that the local church is an insane asylum. When we are fools for Christ the church will be a soft place for healing. We are all in process. Certainly truth is immortal and the church must stand for the truth of the word of God.

In our standing for truth though, we should never forget to kneel with sinners. From the perspective of God, we are all equally in need of mercy. He has showered it upon us. His mercy in the baptism of faith rains down like the torrential flood of Noah's day which covered the earth. Both washed away sin. Both restored. Both gave opportunities for a new start. Noah's flood was corporate in nature, affecting the whole earth and the entire human race. In the baptism of faith, we are cleansed individually and brought corporately into the body of Christ.

Faith has an individual aspect. Surely no one can be saved from their sin and brokenness apart from individually believing in Christ by faith. God's grace is available to those who would individually receive it. However, we are not alone. The body of Christ represented by churches, big and small, is the place where healing takes place. At least it is supposed to be. When our churches become places for bickering, backbiting, gossip, judgment, and personal agendas take center stage, they cease to be healing communities and would serve the world better as parking lots. Mercy is the chief trait of the Church which Jesus founded.

We are never more like God than when we are merciful to others. If we want to have the ability to extend the kind of radical mercy to others that God extends to us it cannot be simply something that we do. It has to be a part of what we are or at the very least, what we are becoming. "Blessed are the merciful for they will be shown mercy" (Matthew 5:7). We are not called to acts of mercy. We are called to be merciful. The merciful acts of our hands flow from the abundance of the mercy which dwells or does not dwell within us.

We are not called by God to do merciful things but to experience a life of cyclic mercy. As God is merciful to us in spite of our imperfections, we extend mercy to others in spite of their imperfections. I am reminded of the first live production I ever watched, The Man of La Mancha, when I was 13 years old. I remember the words of the main character, Don Quixote, when he says "He preaches well who lives well. That is all the divinity I know." As God moves in us, He moves through us.

In early centuries, Christians did not refer to themselves as Christians but as "Followers of the Way." They identified with Christ as followers of the way of the Master of Mercy. Early believers understood the value of strapping on their sandals and picking up their walking stick and following simply after Christ as they sojourned through this life on a pilgrimage of faith. Fellow Pilgrim, though the roads be dusty and our hands be callused from traversing the canyons, roads, and byways of our journey, mercy showing is a matter of the heart.

I have two fairly untamed, high-spirited, and adorable little boys taking up residence with Christina and me. While it is they who have invaded and conquered my life, my home, and my heart, often it feels as though I live in their house! I never cease to be amazed at their ability to "restore" my home to their preferred grubby state, only moments after their devoted mother has cleaned it. Indeed, Sebastian, age four at the time of writing this work, and two-year-old Ephram, are well on their way to owning their own demolition business!

Recently, the "wolf pack" (as I refer to them) was thirsty, after a morning of decorating the fire place with stickers, wrestling with one another, and smiling cutely, so that all would be forgiven. I went to the cupboard to gather a straw cup for the older child and a tumbler cup for the younger. As I poured juice into the first cup I noticed that the cup was cracked and leaking. I was rather surprised to learn that the same was true of the second cup.

Upon inspecting nearly every child's cup in the cabinet, my wife and I realized that nearly a third of the cups, or the straws for them, had cracks and leaks of varying degrees. Apparently these two little happy-maniacs had managed to render a significant number of their cups inoperable. In that moment, it seemed to me as though every cup was broken. They were rendered less than perfectly usable by the rough use of my well intentioned but rambunctious sons. How much like those cups are we?

The world around us can be wildly untamed. The people in our lives, though often well intentioned, drop us, spill us out on the pavement, throw us, or absentmindedly leave us behind when something more amusing catches their eye. We all have cracks. Some are emotional. A few are psychological. Many are spiritual. Some of our cracks even bear witness to the world of our internal pain through the blatancy of external scars. We are all broken.

In John 2:1-11 is recorded the account of Jesus turning the water into wine. This is the first recorded miracle of Jesus in the gospel accounts. It is basically a private miracle. John 2:9-10 make it clear that those who drank the wine were not aware of what Jesus had done. In fact, they praised the bridegroom for bringing out the best wine last! The Bible records that a major part of the importance of the miracles of Jesus was to confirm His identity (John 10:25).

Why then did Jesus perform this miracle, at least in some sense, privately? The answer is found in verse 11. "This, the first of his miraculous signs, Jesus performed at Cana in Galilee. He thus revealed his glory, and his disciples put their faith in him." (John 2:11 NIV) In turning the water into wine, Jesus did approve the institution of marriage. Perhaps this miracle also contains a teaching about the joy of the new wine, the new life, which has come through faith in Jesus Christ. While these and other interpretations of this miracle have merit, a plain reading of the text tells us that this miracle was chiefly for the disciples. It was for them to see the glory of Jesus and fittingly, to place their faith in Him.

Just like the cups in my cabinet, all of us are at some point, to some extent, to varying degrees, just like those disciples of Jesus; in need of the personal miracle of Jesus. Just like those disciples, we are all desperately in need of seeing Jesus for who He is. He is glorious! He is marvelous! His beauty and matchless worth are too great for our minds to comprehend. The truth of it is too vast for our hearts to bear!

We are all in need of continued and ongoing healing. Salvation places us perfectly in Christ but we still reside in this world. The hands of this world still routinely rough us up with careless throws, inadvertent drops, and even intentional spills. Jesus stands ready to heal all who will receive the truth of who He is. Dear unbeliever, won't you trust in the One who loves you enough to lay down His life for you? Dear Christian, why do you toil so? Why do you carry burdens that are not yours to bear on your own? (Matthew 11:28-30)

In Revelation 3:20 Jesus says, "Here I am! I stand at the door and knock. If anyone hears my voice and opens the door, I will come in and eat with him, and he with me." Jesus stands able, present, willing, even longing to transform our brokenness and sorrow. If we place our faith in Him, He will redeem our disappointment. He will use it for God's ultimate glory and our ultimate good, insomuch as we find our ultimate satisfaction in glorifying Him!

Dear child of God, we are all broken. Recognition of this reality helps us to love, and not judge, one another. We are all in need of grace. Acknowledgment of our brokenness is not a weakness, as some perceive weakness. It is the gift of God. It is only when we recognize how deep our need that we will know how vast is His love! "No, in all these things we are more than conquerors through him who loved us. For I am convinced that neither death nor life, neither angels nor demons, neither the present nor the future, nor any powers, neither height nor depth, nor anything else in all creation, will be able to separate us from the love of God that is in Christ Jesus our Lord" (Romans 8:37-39).

Chapter 6

"Blessed are the pure in heart, for they will see God."
(Matthew 5:8)

In early childhood I was raised almost exclusively by my mother. Among my younger uncles and cousins I guess you could say I was the momma's boy, the whiner, and generally not as tough as the other boys. The summer between my third and fourth grade year in school, my youngest uncle, who is five years older than me, and I spent the summer at my aunt's house with my cousin who is my age. I remember visits to that little town of Cottage Grove, Oregon fondly. It is surrounded by lakes, rivers, and forest. It is a curious child's paradise.

One afternoon a large group of family and friends went swimming in a popular local swimming hole at the nearby Sharps Creek recreation area. The "natural dam" is a huge rock wall which creates a natural waterfall in a river a few miles out of town. At the top of the fall, the water is fairly shallow. People swim in the pools created here. Others jump from the top of this more than fifty foot waterfall. On this day, I was determined that I would jump from the top of the cliff, plummeting into the cool waters below.

After watching some of the adults jump off of the cliff in to the water, I was filled with confidence. I barged in front of the other children who were hesitating to jump. I said, "I'll do it!" I stepped past them and out onto the edge of the precipice. When I looked down at the jagged rocks below my courage melted! I was terrified. In what was surely less than a few moments I had an internal battle similar to that which we have all had at times in our life. Though I probably did not articulate it in that way, I thought that this isn't safe. I will not be secure. This is not sane!

I remember the peace came into me all of the sudden when I said to myself, "It's time to jump, that's the long and the short of it." I leapt with all of my might and plummeted down; hanging in the air in deafening silence for what my memory tells me felt like minutes, then "splash!" The cool water rushed over me, I was beneath the water, and then my body broke the surface, I emerged victorious over the fear which would have had me to forever forego the experience of letting go.

In the instant that I let go of my fear and jumped, I experienced what I believe to be something very much akin to the purity of the heart of which Jesus speaks in Matthew 5:8. "Blessed are the pure in heart, for they will see God." In that instant I knew purity of intention. My young mind was completely clear of clutter. The world around me faded away. My family, and the fact that I was not known as the courageous one, grew faint and unimportant. Silence enveloped me and for that instant there was just me, the real me, the uncomplicated me who is unencumbered by external expectations, the cliff, and the river.

All of our platitudes, social clichés, pride, accomplishments, religion, are but clever disguises that mask the pure self who is hiding beneath the surface of the external self. We constantly put on a show for the world to see. Conversely, the world around us constantly pushes and shoves us into boxes of expectation. We are at war with ourselves and the world around us fuels us with the ammunition to wage the war! The pure in heart shall see God because they will not allow clever disguises of religious piety or supposed strength to stop them from standing naked, stripped of vanity before God.

If we are to experience the fullness of God's presence in our lives, we must allow our feet to leave the earth. We must come to the edge of the cliff of faith and jump. How many believers fail to know the fullness of God's love in the innermost parts of their being for lack of willingness to step out of our safe comfort zones, let go of the false security of this world, and judge sanity not by man's rational thoughts but according to the word of God? It is indeed uncomfortable to forgo the ground for the moment of falling. It is not for the sky that we leap, however, the excitement of that moment fades. It is in order to bathe in the deep waters of the grace of God's pure love.

Standing at the edge of the cliff we gaze into the unknown. What will happen if I jump in completely? What will people think of me if I give myself over fully to Christ? If I go down under the depth of the water will I ever return? Standing on the cliff is safe. In the air there is abandonment. In the water, my friend, there is refreshment and life! Jesus has not invited us to live safe "religious" lives. He has invited us to participate in the wonderful glory of His Father. He has made a way for us to know God in the fullest sense.

We will never experience the freedom of God that comes in abandonment, standing on the cliff. Our clever religious practices will never bring peace, only counterfeit comfort. In the Beatitudes, Jesus is primarily spelling out for us the way of the lover of God. His teaching stands horribly juxtaposed to that of the Pharisee of His day and the heart of the Pharisee which remains in our day. A focus of the heart toward outward purity is a snare, a trap which lures us in with its promise of purity but only delivers the vilest pretense of false sanctity.

I recall one sunny afternoon when I was thirteen years old and had only recently moved to Butte, Montana. I lived there for a couple of years during high school with my father and grandfather. One afternoon I was exploring a very old log cabin style garage on the back of the property where we lived. It was a neat old building which was just chock full of fun things for a thirteen year old kid to get into. I found this old white porcelain bowl and what appeared to be a water pitcher. Both were very old and apparently stained by age. I took both of them out of the old garage and began to fill them up with water from the hose that I would then pour on my rather unoriginally named little dog, Bingo.

After I had been at this a while, playing with the old water pitcher and the dog, I overheard my grandfather telling my dad to tell me to stop messing with that pitcher and put it back in the old garage. My dad asked him why and he explained, "that thing is filthy! It is an old chamber pot!" Only he had another, more vulgar name for the chamber pot. In Matthew 23:25-28 Jesus tells the Pharisees that they have radically missed the mark. So have we.

Rather than cleaning the inside of their hearts which would lead to outward devotion, they only focused on the appearance of holiness. They have replaced the heart's pure devotion, the heart's pure cry to be filled with the very presence of God with an outward commitment to religious ritual, custom, and practice. They have cleaned the outside of the cup but drank up the vilest drink of pride, hypocrisy, and self-exaltation.

They are like the soldier who has mirror-like spit-shined boots, a perfect hair cut which he trims daily, a uniform that can stand up by itself because of the bucket of starch he used before ironing, but inside he lacks any sense of devotion to his task. He is outwardly praised but when trouble comes he will be the first to run. When we lack the pure heart of reckless abandon to the sovereign love of our Heavenly Father, we are likewise outwardly dressed for the spiritual battles of life but inwardly not more than a moment away from fleeing.

A pure heart is one given over to God in simplicity, whatever comes. Our spiritual eyes are opened when, and only when, we stop working from the outside in and begin to allow God to work on us from the inside out. The pure in heart are those who have allowed God to work within them to transform them. We will never be perfect (perfect tense - presently) in this life but we are being perfected (active tense – actively) at all times in this life. God always was, always is, and always will be, at work within us.

We are all growing, all becoming. None has become. I like to think that my heart is pure. The reality is that I know what a pretender that I can also be . When addressing the subject of outward religious trapping, prideful cleverness, I am writing from experience. I know how vain my heart can be. I know fully that you and I have been wounded in this life and often the show that we put on for the world around us is to mask and cover the pain that lies within. The world trains us well how to treat it.

My journey into the Marine Corps was spurred by many ambitions. I genuinely wanted to serve the great land which had given me so many opportunities in spite of coming from fairly humble beginnings. I wanted access to training and a college education. I wanted to be a part of something bigger than myself. All of that is true. However, when I strip away all of that and consider my heart of hearts, it becomes clear that my primary motivation for joining the Marine Corps was that this child of a single mother wanted to prove that he was a better man that his father. It is really that simple.

I loved being a Marine. I often say that when I looked in the mirror as a nineteen-year-old Marine I saw a ten-foot tall bulletproof superhero. My heart was swollen with pride and my mind was singly focused on accomplishment. I had an excellent enlisted career. I was promoted quickly. I had an excellent reputation among my peers and superiors. During my first enlistment I commanded an Amphibious Assault Vehicle, an amphibious tank. I was a Marine's Marine. A stalwart young man who believed he could do anything. In many ways I was a fool.

I sensed a call to ministry very early in my faith journey. As a newly converted teenager I knew that the Lord had called me to ministry. To say that the calling to ministry terrified me is like saying that the molten lava is a little bit warm. God never let me go. Through various ways He kept calling and tugging on my heart until finally I was broken and had to answer His call. He sent a precious man into my life. He is the retired father of a friend who was a part time preacher at local nursing homes and retirement communities.

I asked Bill Ellerman if he would mentor me so that I could start to prepare for entering the ministry fourteen years from then, after I retired from the military. He told me that he would do one better than that. He told me that I was coming to the nursing home with him that week and to bring a sermon because I was preaching! Filled with feelings of inadequacy for the task I did as he instructed and delivered my first sermon. The contents of my sermon were jumbled and scattered that day but the purity of my heart was not.

Standing in the pulpit of that little chapel in that retirement community in Yuma, Arizona, it was as though I was back on that cliff in Oregon. I jumped off again. I took one giant leap over the edge, leaving behind my safety, my security, and my sanity. I chose not to define success in this life by the common standards of the world around me. I began preaching anywhere that they would let me. I soon found my way to Crossroads Mission where I preached weekly to homeless, and recently homeless men in their life recovery program.

One evening after I had been ministering there for a few months I pulled up on a particularly dry and searing desert evening. I stepped out of my dusty bronco and began to walk inside to the makeshift chapel in the cafeteria. As I walked through the doors of the place I was struck by the most pungent odor. Many of the men to whom I preached were presently homeless. Some wore filthy clothing. Others reeked of alcohol. That evening the smell was particularly overpowering or perhaps my senses were especially acute.

Whatever the cause, my senses were overwhelmed. I thought, "What am I doing here? Why not go somewhere else where the smell is better." I am embarrassed to say that I literally stopped dead in my tracks and almost walked right out of that place. Then I sensed the presence of God in an uncommon way. The next thought that flooded my mind, washing into my soul, was a vision of Jesus ministering to the lepers, to the outcasts, loving the unlovely. If Jesus were to have been preaching His message anywhere in that city, that night, in that desert, He would have been right there!

Pride was written on my heart. The love of God crushed it! How easily the pomp of our own accomplishments causes us to lose focus, to abandon the purity of the heart which yearns to do the will of our Father! How easily we are drawn into pride. How desperately fickle is the human soul. Outward appearances, whatever they may be, don't impress God and they surely don't bring us peace. This is what Jesus was saying to the rich young ruler in Luke 18:22, "When Jesus heard this, he said to him, "You still lack one thing. Sell everything you have and give to the poor, and you will have treasure in heaven. Then come, follow me."

He wasn't condemning his wealth directly. He was saying to get rid of, to sell, anything and everything that muddles the purity of our heart. Dear child of God, get off of the cliff. Jump into the fullness of the love of God. He loves us with such reckless abandon. Why are we so slow to respond in like fashion? Leap! And in leaping find your solid footing on the foundation of God's wild love for you and me!

Chapter 7

"Blessed are the peacemakers, for they will be called sons of God." (Matthew 5:9)

The sweeping love with which God pursues us is the most powerful force in the universe. The paradox of the God who created all things, pouring out love and mercy to us who are smaller than the tiniest of insects by comparison, is unfathomable. The violence of the Cross of Christ which brought us peace with God is the greatest dichotomy that I can envision. Imagine, the King of glory bruised, battered, beaten, and nailed to tree – for you and me. This is unbelievable and yet we are empowered to believe it through the gift of faith.

When I conceive of such wonder, I feel like a child half awake, hovering somewhere between the reality I know and a dream. I become lost in the mystery of God's glory veiled in human flesh, on a tree, hanging on the Cross to die in order that I might live. There are those who make war for the sake of violence. There are those who seek peace in a whimsical fashion, naïve to the cruelty this often reigns on earth. Then there is Christ, who shattered evil and brought peace through the shame and suffering of the Cross.

Peace in this broken world always comes at a price. I am inclined to believe that pure pacifism is the untenable philosophy of those who would enjoy freedom at another person's expense, though in a very real sense, all believers everywhere enjoy the freedom of God's love at the expense of the sacrifice of Jesus Christ. Liberty in the religious, social, and national sphere always comes with the shedding of blood. Seldom does a violent dictator or cruel tyrant abdicate his throne peacefully simply because it is the will of the people. This was the case with Hitler and it was also the case with our enemy, the Devil.

Consider the Cross. It was the violence of the Cross which secured peace with God for humanity. At the Cross Jesus purchased for us a grace born in earnest brutality. God uses violent actions in the Old Testament to accomplish His will in the immediate situation and in order to further unfold His plan of redemption. In the Bible violence is not absent. It always has a redeeming quality greater than its immediate unfolding. The road to redemption is often paved in violence but the unmitigated violence of the world often leaves us battle worn and scarred.

Most of us carry deep wounds from the battles of this life; we are all, in a very real sense, wounded worshipers. We worship a God of healing and restoration. We follow our Lord who heals with broken hands. He reached out during Jesus' earthly ministry, He was busy bringing healing, and He is still healing lives to this very day. Matthew 4:23 says, "Jesus went throughout Galilee, teaching in their synagogues, preaching the good news of the kingdom, and healing every disease and sickness among the people."

During His earthly ministry He brought healing. Even now, Jesus reaches out to us with wounded hands and His love invites us to bring our wounds to Him for healing. We are at war in this world. In our homes we are often at war with each other. In our churches battles rage. Within ourselves the war against sin and despair rolls on day after day. Worship Him with your wounds. There is redemption in suffering. God offers peace through the sacrifice of our pain at the altar of redemption.

Jesus went to the Cross to make peace for us with God. We are called likewise to go into the world and make known that offer to mankind. Jesus waged war against sin using the sword of truth and the sling of grace. He confronted sin openly and unapologetically. So should we. He also motivated people to embrace the love of God. He made peace with God on our behalf by suffering for us, not waging war against us. Do we wage our battles likewise?

I must be on every email forward list in existence. Not long ago I received an email from a certain Christian organization which was calling on pastors to encourage their congregants to boycott a very well-known restaurant chain for its supposed stand on a particular hot-button political issue, the issue of same sex marriage. The trouble with a boycott of this type, as I see it, is that a company does not have a voice as such. It is made up of many individuals with varying political and religious ideologies.

The spokesperson for the company has a voice which reflects the opinions of the leadership of the corporation, but what of the countless employees of this restaurant chain who are merely working to earn a living? Do they have a voice? Did the corporation poll all of its employees to find out what their views on this divisive issue are? I very much suspect that they did not. Restaurant chains do not have opinions. People have opinions.

In this email, same sex marriage was referred to over and over again as SSM, which, previously unbeknownst to me, has apparently been adopted as the official acronym. I served several years in the military prior to entering the ministry. Seeing this acronym over and over again in this boycott solicitation email reminded me very much of the military's over usage of acronyms. Acronyms have a way of dehumanizing whatever they refer to. It occurs to me that their repetitive and long term use also allows us to forget the human element of this controversial issue.

Here is another acronym; PAC, Political Action Committee. Is that what the Church of Christ has been reduced to? It seems that, at times, the Church looks much less like Christ on the Cross than it should and much more like a Political Action Committee at election time than it ought. I am certainly not saying that the Church should not be involved in social issues. What I am saying is that when we are involved in social issues we should take care to

79

always look like Christ. For example, what looks more like Christ, picketing an abortion clinic or loving a young girl through a pregnancy, giving her shelter, clothes, and food so she has an alternative to the abortion readily available?

This particular boycott may even have some merit. That is not my point. I am much more concerned with what appears to me to be the willingness, even the preference, on the part of the Church to forfeit looking like Jesus in our battles in favor of looking so much like just another entity of the world. It is as though in our very efforts to fight the ideological wars of this age we are boycotting the love of Christ. Jesus ate with sinners as a way of loving them into the Kingdom of God. He did not make picket signs against their sin. He loved them in spite of their sin, and even died to forgive their sin.

I am deeply saddened that Christianity has been reduced by so many to merely another social ideology, yet another encampment on the landscape of an already scarred, bruised, and overpopulated culture war. Christians have not been called to be culture warriors as such; we have been called to be active participants in God's plan of redemption and grace in this world! Our task as believers is not primarily to go on the offensive against opposing worldviews as much as it is to aggressively love others with the radical, unending, unrelenting love of Christ! We do well not to define ourselves according to what we are not but according to what we are.

Boycott if you choose to do so but in all that you do, as a follower of Jesus Christ, remember that we have been called to look like Christ, act like Christ, and love like Christ! The Church, while being a large and influential organization, is so much more than that. We are the hands through which God embraces this hurting generation and world. Above all, let us never boycott the radical love of Christ; let us focus primarily on loving people into the Kingdom of God rather than boycotting them out of it.

The calling of God is to be a living reflection of the love of Jesus Christ. In Matthew 5:16 Jesus says, "In the same way, let your light shine before others, so that they may see your good works and give glory to your Father who is in heaven." When I was a kid growing up in Northern California, one of my favorite places to visit was Mirror Lake in Yosemite Valley. Mirror Lake gets its name from the fact that from the right perspective and during the right time of year, it proudly displays a spectacular reflection of Mt. Watkins.

The mountain is flawlessly reflected in the lake! In the Gospel of Matthew, Jesus admonishes us to let the light of the love of God which is inside of us shine so that others will see it and give glory to God. The light which is inside of us is the light of that love which God expressed at the Cross. As we draw near to the Cross this Lenten Season, let us consider the breadth of God's love and mercy which was demonstrated at the Cross in the person of Jesus Christ. God's love shouts to us from Cross, "Come all you who are heavy laden and I will give you rest!" (Matthew 11:28) God's love shouts through us to a world in need of mercy and grace as we allow our lives to reflect the love of God that was demonstrated at the Cross – just as Mirror Lake reflects the mountain!

We are peacemakers when we proclaim in our actions and our words the love of God with Christ-likeness at the center. The church strives for peace most fully when it is at war with the things that Jesus was (is) at war with and when we fight the battles the way Jesus did (does)! Where are the picket signs boycotting judgment? We must speak the truth in love. Stand firm for the truth. Contend for the faith. Wage this battle like Jesus did, loving the unlovely, reconciling men to God by waging war for the sake of securing peace.

Chapter 8

"Blessed are those who are persecuted because of righteousness, for theirs is the kingdom of heaven."
(Matthew 5:10)

Whether it is modern day Christians in fundamentalist Islamic regions, Dietrich Bonheoffer and the confessing Church of Hitler's Germany, or the earliest of Roman Christians, persecution has always accompanied Gospel. It is persecution, not material blessings, that often marks the life of true believers. The world always rejects what is true. The world hates the truth of the Gospel because it shines a light on the evil that the world calls the good. People lost in their sins most often have terribly little interest in having those sins exposed by the light of truth.

In John 3:19-21 Jesus says, "This is the verdict: Light has come into the world, but men loved darkness instead of light because their deeds were evil. Everyone who does evil hates the light, and will not come into the light for fear that his deeds will be exposed. But whoever lives by the truth comes into the light, so that it may be seen plainly that what he has done has been done through God."

In our day, in our land, we do not know the horror of persecution as did the early church. While the early church was seeking to establish itself, it was confronted by the worst kind of atrocities. Our age is different. We see the crumbling edifice of many closed down city and rural churches as the evidence that what was once well-established is, in many ways, crumbling all around us. Some of those attacks are from within. They come from the always present temptation toward apathy and indifference in our spiritual lives.

Our children's worldview is shaped by what they are taught in an increasingly secularized public school system. They are further influenced by the media and mainstream ideology of a culture which has rejected the authority of God, ridiculed His revealed word, the Bible, and worse yet, and has forgone even the notion that there is such a thing as absolute truth. These are desperate times. However, if we believe that these times are any more desperate than the times in which the church was incepted, we deceive ourselves. Imagine the disciples who watched Jesus be crucified and buried.

Are these times more desperate than the three days that Jesus spent in the tomb? What of the Roman persecutions? What of the times of the Reformation when Gospel confessing believers were martyred for truth? In many ways these are perhaps unprecedented times. My desire is not to minimize the present day version of persecution which the church faces. My point is merely to say that the church has always faced trials and through trials it was established and has grown. We are supposed to be just as faithful, just as committed, just as fervent about evangelism and missions; just as radical as the persecuted church has ever been here in our own day.

We are our own worst enemy. We fight the wrong fights. We are constantly engaged in the wrong battles. The early church, for example was persecuted for proclaiming the truth. Often in the modern day we are "persecuted" by a culture which rejects the truth that we have failed to live out. School prayer is important. Indeed. I am perplexed, however that the volume of time spent fighting for school prayer likely outweighs the time spent on the part of the crusaders in personal devotional prayer. Why is our focus on ensuring that we can pray publicly when we don't pray privately?

I agree that public prayer should be protected. I greatly support the free liberties of religious expression that the founders of this great nation wove into the founding documents. I am not condemning protecting public prayer. My point is more directly that I am convinced that the Church is often more concerned with shedding light than living in the light. Persecution is the byproduct of living and proclaiming the Gospel. First, let us go into our prayer closets and win the battle over self which keeps us from praying with earnestness and regularity. Then, when the battle is won in private, let us take that peace of God which we found in prayer inwardly into whatever arena where we find ourselves placed. Fight the battles of this age if you must but not before fighting the inward and eternal battles.

There is a cave that I love to visit in Northern California. Moaning Caverns is just a short drive from where I was raised in Modesto, California. It is an easy day trip that we made many times as a family growing up and even visited on school field trips routinely. You can either descend through a hole in the top of the cavern on a rappel rope or take the safe (sane) route down a very large spiral staircase. I have always chosen the staircase. Upon reaching the bottom of the deep and twisting cavern, the tour guide will turn off the artificial lighting and ask everyone to keep silent. In the deepest of darkness the sound of an underground river can be heard faintly in the distance moving through the rock underfoot. It is the darkest of darkness, there deep in the heart of the earth.

The depth of our sin and brokenness is only revealed by the glorious light of the holiness of God! As one ascends from the darkness of the cavern the wondrous light of a Northern California Sierra Nevada mountainous sky floods the eye. Often the intensity of the light is so dazzling that your eyes need time to adjust and the smell of the pine is so beautiful that the sensory feast is overwhelming. As we consider the darkness of our sin and fallen state in the light of the glory of the love of God as demonstrated in Jesus Christ, I am likewise overwhelmed by the loveliness, exquisiteness, and the magnificence of the grace that He has shown us.

Dear friends, if we are to be the people which God has called us to be we must stop shining flashlights from our caves! Consider the words of Jesus. "Why do you look at the speck of sawdust in your brother's eye and pay no attention to the plank in your own eye? How can you say to your brother, 'Let me take the speck out of your eye,' when all the time there is a plank in your own eye? You hypocrite, first take the plank out of your own eye, and then you will see clearly to remove the speck from your brother's eye" (Matthew 7:3-5). If we would get busy loving the world radically rather than fighting culture wars with them vehemently, they would want what we have.

When our places of faith are healing communities where we are all becoming like Christ and no one assumes they have already become perfected, the world will be drawn into these places out of their desperate longing for the tenderness of God expressed in us. Protecting the crumbling edifices of our half-empty churches by fighting against the tide of secularism is far less Christ-like and fruitful than laying down our crusader equipment in order to embrace the world.

We don't need more crusades which create the appearance of persecution which is merely rejection of our perceived ideology. Should believers engage in moral and ethical crises? Certainly. However, we must suffer for Christ if we are to proclaim Him to this lost and dying generation! We have got to set aside secondary matters in order to contend for the faith. We must primarily be witnesses to the beauty and peace of God. One who suffers for Christ sets aside personal preference, non-Gospel essentials, in order to build His body and love the world. One who suffers for Christ counts her own comfort a distant second to the work of building the kingdom.

Church history affirms that in fact persecution, suffering for Christ, builds the Church. Whether in ancient Rome or in modern-day Communist China, when the Church is persecuted it grows. It is as though the pressure of persecution is necessary for the Church to truly flourish. When the Church becomes too comfortable, Christians become complacent and the Church loses spiritual intensity. From the very foundations of the Church, persecution has built the Church.

In Acts 5:41 we read that the Apostles rejoiced that they had been counted worthy to share in the sufferings of Christ. The Apostles had the perspective that when they were persecuted it was an honor to be counted worthy of such persecution. What would give the Apostles such a strong and abiding conviction that they would not only be willing but honored to suffer for righteousness sake? What kind of fool would count themselves worthy to suffer for the name of Christ? How can it be joy to be counted worthy of such suffering?

Only a fool for Christ counts it joy to suffer as He suffered for His sake and His ultimate glory. When the glory of God is central in the life of a follower of Jesus, the wisdom of this world fades as if it were nothing. The power of the resurrection of Christ filled them with supernatural power and with great courage. The power of Christ's miracles was not enough to give them total and complete faith in Him. Even having seen the miracles, they did not completely understand who it was that they followed.

The fire in their hearts that was quenched by the crucifixion was ignited hot enough in the resurrection to charge a light that burns to this very day. Where fear had taken up residence, faith took over. Not a whispered faith which is quieted in persecution and trials, but a raging faith which could not be stilled. What is it that gives a man or a woman the courage to face persecution and even death? It is in the risen Lord Jesus Christ. If Jesus had died on the Cross and not risen from the dead, the disciples would probably still be hiding in that house in Jerusalem! It was faith in Christ because He had risen from the dead that empowered them.

Faith in and of itself is powerless. It is a trite philosophy at best to suggest that faith in anything has the power to provide meaning and purpose and power for one's life. For faith to have meaning it must have an object. In other words, it is not faith that changes things. Faith is the vehicle that we use to connect to the power of

Jesus Christ. He changes us. Not the early Church Fathers, the Early Church, the Pilgrim Separatists, nor the scores of modern Christians who are persecuted around the world were or are empowered by vague faith. They are empowered by the presence of the resurrected Christ in their lives!

Courage is not the absence of fear but the presence of trust in God. It is not possible to negate fear by forgoing it. It cannot be so easily dismissed. It must be demolished by faith, which is trust. The risen Lord Jesus Chris is worthy of our trust. The early Church had power to face persecution because they were full of faith in God. We have access to the same power to conquer fear. It was the resurrection power that enabled the Early Church and the apostles. In Romans 8:17 the Apostle Paul writes, "Now if we are children, then we are heirs – heirs of God and co-heirs with Christ, if indeed we share in his sufferings in order that we may also share in his glory." In I Corinthians 4:10 he writes that we are "fools for Christ!"

It is a matter of perspective and I would suggest that the American Church in general could stand to receive a healthy dose of that perspective which is found in the pages of the Bible. The great trouble is that we have forgotten what the church is for. What I am saying is that we are too comfortable in our seats. The world is crying out all around us that it cannot go on unless we get up out of our pews. The apostles were fools for Christ. Should we be any different? The early Church was so full of the resurrection power of Christ that they were willing to abandon everything for His sake. Have we been called to anything less?

Jesus said that the persecuted were blessed. He did not say that we should avoid persecution at all costs and then call that commonplace, smug complacency, which fills our churches, to pass for Christianity. The grand problem is that we have forgotten what the church is for. The geography of First Congregational Church of Peru, Illinois serves well to illustrate this point. The church that I shepherd is located in the center of its city. It is encircled by the local post office, Red Cross, police station, fire station, and the area hospital.

I fear greatly that the underlying problem in many churches, which surfaces as near constant power struggles, petty conflicts of all types, and a general unwillingness to give ourselves over completely to the work of Christ, is that we have become institutionalized. The early Church was persecuted in its infancy. The modern western church crumbles in its golden years. We have grown weak by our lack of persecution! We are like the boxer who loses stamina and balance because he has not gotten into the ring for many years.

Many in the mainstream culture have grown so comfortable with the towering edifices of our churches that the uniqueness of the Gospel is lost on them. It is often lost on us as well. Churches dot the landscape. They are seen by many as just one more institution of the community. People with no connection to any church routinely come to me seeking money. They go to the local welfare office, and then the food pantries, then they swing by the church in the afternoon.

When pressed about their relationship with Jesus Christ and their connection to His Church, they stare perplexed. They do not know what one has to do with the other. Often, we don't either. We proclaim allegiance with God's will and yet in our actions we openly and many times knowingly willingly, contradict the purpose of the church. The Church has a unique mission which is completely unlike any agency in society. We are not the Red Cross. While they have a great social mission and help many people with personal needs in disaster recovery, they can never rectify the disaster that sin has wrought upon this earth.

The post office delivers messages of all types. What is our message? Some churches tell the world of God's holiness to the exclusion of His grace and mercy. Sadly, many others proclaim grace without definition. They send the message of sentimental love apart from the weight of the cost of God's love – the sacrifice of this life for Christ in response of the sacrifice of Christ for eternal life. Suffice it to say that belief in the Gospel of Jesus Christ is a far more worthy and weighty subject than merely purchasing celestial fire insurance at the cost of a pittance of second-rate faith.

The police provide the community with security but only Christ offers eternal security by abandonment, faith, to the will of the Father. The hospital heals for a time but only the Church has the message of everlasting hope and eternal restoration in Christ. My friends, God is calling us to be the uniquely instituted covenantal community of healing that He intended for His Church. The greatest enemy of the Gospel is complacency in the relative comfort and religious freedom that western society affords.

The greatest calling of the body of Christ is to cast off the preoccupations with pseudo-Gospels of various forms and embrace the unique call of God to be the people of God. Our chief aim is to proclaim His glory and declare His mighty works of salvation. Often as I put my sons to sleep, just before they doze off to sleep, they will say "Daddy, are you there?" "Yes, son, I'm here." The knowledge of their abba's presence, their daddy's presence, is enough to secure within them the comfort necessary to turn over and go to sleep, without a thought of harm.

Our Heavenly Father is with us, close to us, empowering us. Our task is to make Him known sincerely, simply, in earnestness. Let us cast off the shackles of pseudo-religious conflicts for the only thing for which His Church was created – the declaration of His ultimate worth for our ultimate joy and His ultimate glory!

Conclusion

There is something spectacular to me about photography. It is fascinating to have the ability to freeze a moment in time with the press of a finger and the snap of a shutter. I once had a photography teacher who said something that changed the way I viewed photography forever. He said "Learn to see light differently." Those simple words are considerably profound. You see, when you look at an object you are not looking at that object at all. You are looking at light which is bouncing off of that object.

What our eyes perceive is the light reflected from the thing, not the thing at all. So it is with the Cross of Christ. Its meaning is lost if we only consider the wood of the beams and the flesh of His body. To fully comprehend the meaning of the Cross we must learn to see light differently. We must learn to see the light of the love of God which is being reflected from the Cross of Jesus Christ. Then as we allow that light to flood our souls, we will be become just like the pictures which I love to take, images of the love and light of Christ!

It is my prayer that through this work you have learned to see the light of Christ a little bit differently. The beatitudes are a alive with the power to transform our lives. "May I never boast except in the cross of our Lord Jesus Christ, through which the world has been crucified to me, and I to the world" (Galatians 6:14).

Scripture Index

Also by Chris Surber

Sweet Potatoes in My Coffee is an inspirational book based on a series of sermons delivered at First Congregational Church by Chris Surber entitled "Living The Grace Filled Life!" The book's title comes from an incident involving the author, his then 15 month old son, some coffee, and some Sweet Potatoes! The grace-filled life is about relating rightly to God as loving Father, relating rightly to one another out of a desire to participate in God's love and grace, and seeing oneself as God sees us; forgiven and free!

Available on Amazon.com.

From Energion Publications

Many Christians struggle with grief. Does grieving show a lack of faith? Where is God in my times of need? Jody Neufeld teams up with social worker Janet Wilkie to provide a practical, positive, faith-filled guide to dealing with grief honestly and effectively. If you or a loved one are dealing with loss, you won't want to miss this little book.

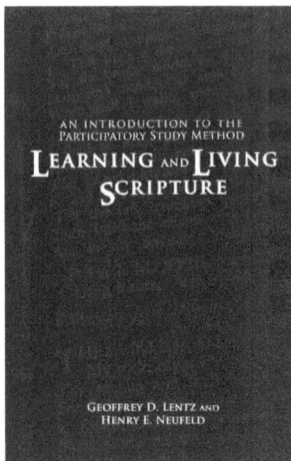

Many Christians struggle with reading the Bible and understanding how it applies to their lives. Learning and Living Scripture starts from the idea that the Bible is God's Word, and that in order to hear God speaking you need to take a different approach than you would with any other type of literature. Combining sound scholarship with a constant sense of the spiritual value of the text, the authors lead you to combine your Bible reading with prayer and worship so that you can commune more deeply with your creator.

More from Energion Publications

Personal Study
The Jesus Paradigm	$17.99
Finding My Way in Christianity	$16.99
When People Speak for God	$17.99
Holy Smoke, Unholy Fire	$14.99
Not Ashamed of the Gospel	$12.99
Evidence for the Bible	$16.99
Christianity and Secularism	$16.99
What's In A Version?	$12.99
Christian Archy	$9.99
The Messiah and His Kingdom to Come	$19.99 (B&W)
(an EnerPower Press title)	$49.99 (Color)

Christian Living
52 Weeks of Ordinary People – Extraordinary God	$7.99
Daily Devotions of Ordinary People – Extraordinary God	$19.99
Directed Paths	$7.99
Grief: Finding the Candle of Light	$8.99
I Want to Pray	$7.99
Soup Kitchen for the Soul	$12.99

Bible Study
Learning and Living Scripture	$12.99
To the Hebrews: A Participatory Study Guide	$9.99
Revelation: A Participatory Study Guide	$9.99
The Gospel According to St. Luke: A Participatory Study Guide	$8.99
Identifying Your Gifts and Service: Small Group Edition	$12.99
Consider Christianity, Volume I & II Study Guides	$7.99 each
Why Four Gospels?	$11.99

Theology
God's Desire for the Nations	$18.99

Fiction
Megabelt	$12.99

Generous Quantity Discounts Available
Dealer Inquiries Welcome
Energion Publications
P.O. Box 841
Gonzalez, FL 32560
Website: http://energionpubs.com
Phone: (850) 525-3916

www.ingramcontent.com/pod-product-compliance
Lightning Source LLC
LaVergne TN
LVHW011213080426
835508LV00007B/754